BRUNEI

S

ARAWAK

ALIMANTA
(BORNEO)

0

Macassar

Bangkalan
    MADURA

BALI    LOMBOK        FI

Denpasar
    Sanur    SUMBAWA

        SUMBA

D1380585

120

10

*Titles in the series*

# The Kris

# The Kris

*Mystic Weapon of the Malay World*

Second Edition

EDWARD FREY

SINGAPORE
OXFORD UNIVERSITY PRESS
OXFORD NEW YORK
1988

*Oxford University Press*

*Oxford New York Toronto*
*Delhi Bombay Calcutta Madras Karachi*
*Petaling Jaya Singapore Hong Kong Tokyo*
*Nairobi Dar es Salaam Cape Town*
*Melbourne Auckland*
*and associated companies in*
*Berlin Ibadan*

*Oxford is a trade mark of Oxford University Press*

© *Oxford University Press Pte. Ltd. 1986, 1988*
*First published 1986*
*Second edition 1988*

*ISBN 0 19 588906 1*

*Printed in Singapore by Kim Hup Lee Printing Co. Pte. Ltd.*
*Published by Oxford University Press Pte. Ltd.,*
*Unit 221, Ubi Avenue 4, Singapore 1440*

# Preface

WHEN I first decided to write a book about the kris, after over thirty years of collecting them, I little dreamed the extent of new knowledge that was there for the searching—particularly for the English-reading scholar willing to probe the mass of material that exists in Dutch, French, German and Indonesian.

As my work got under way with translators of these languages, I soon saw that I was entering a new and splendid area of art appreciation little known to the Western world but alive and vibrant in Indonesia and Malaysia. Travels to Bali, Java, and Malaysia in quest of new knowledge affirmed even more that the kris is a living cultural object, dear to the hearts and profound in the respect of the peoples of these two countries.

Then came the day at a luncheon table of museum people in New Delhi when I was invited by S. Stronge of the Victoria and Albert Museum to come to London and study the krises in their collection. Of course I accepted this invitation, and that visit proved to be the opening of another new world in my studies—a world of precious objects there for the touching and close inspection, the grace of patterned wood and steel, the mystery of god-like images, and the wonder of the magic properties attributed to the pieces.

Now I knew that I must make my contribution to that of all those before me, and for those who love Indonesian art as I do.

In this book I use the Western spelling 'kris' rather than the Malay form 'keris'—except when quoting Malay terms. In the great body of Western literature, kris is the form invariably used. As modern researchers become more global, there is a tendency to adopt native spellings; however, I see no good reason to change the spelling of a word that has been spelled kris for more than 150 years. There is much to support this decision:

Marsden, in his *Dictionary of the Malay Language* (1812), converting directly from Arabic (jawi) spelling to English, spells it *kris*; Crawfurd's *Grammar and Dictionary of Malay Language* (1852), has it *kris*, and so do Raffles (1817), Wallace (1869), McNair (1882), Burton (1884), Forbes (1885) (*kriss*), Cool (1897), Skeat (1900) (*kriss*), Groneman (1910), Huyser (1918) (*kriss*), Holstein (1930), Jasper and Pirngadie (1930), Buttin (1933) (*kriss*), Stone (1934), Rassers (1940), Wagner (1959), and Pant (1980).

Gardner, Hill, Woolley and Griffith-Williams, all of whom were published in Singapore between 1936 and 1956, use the form *keris*, as does Solyum writing from Java in 1978.

Since *keris* is actually pronounced *kris*, just as *kereta* (carriage) is pronounced *kreh-ta*, I favour the more phonetic spelling with its overwhelming literary tradition.

Many people have helped me in the creation of this book and I am grateful to all of them. I thank Robert Skelton and Susan Stronge of the Victoria and Albert Museum, B. Durrans at the British Museum of Mankind; Bennet Bronson of the Field Museum in Chicago; Constance Sheares and Marianne Teo of the National Museum in Singapore; J. H. van Brakel at the Tropen Museum in Amsterdam; Ian Ave, Mr van der Wilk, Arman De Guemenee, all of Rijksmuseum voor Volkenkunde in Leiden; and Gayatri Pant of the National Museum in New Delhi. Also of great help to me were kris experts Robert Hales of London and H. B. Hardiono of Surabaya, Java. I am forever changed for the association and friendships I have made with these people.

*Mansfield, Ohio, 1985*　　　　　　　　　　　　EDWARD FREY
*Singapore, 1988*

# Contents

# Sources of Illustrations

British Museum of Mankind, London
  Figure 11f
  Plates 6a, b, 10b

Field Museum of Natural History, Chicago
  Figures 11j, l
  Plates 2a, 13b

H. B. Hardiono, Surabaya, Indonesia
  Figures 10c, f, h, j, 11d
  Plates 8a, 11a, b, c, d, 15b

Musée de l'Homme, Paris
  Plate 2b

Rijksmuseum voor Volkenkunde, Leiden
  Plates 4a, 5a, b, c, 6c, 7a, 15a

National Museum, Singapore
  Figures 11e, g, 12a, b

Tropen Museum, Amsterdam
  Figures 5, 10d, e, h, i, 11c
  Plates 9b, 14a, b, c

Victoria and Albert Museum, London
  Plates 7b, c

Victoria University, Wellington, New Zealand
  Plate 4b

Author's Collection
  Figures 1, 6, 7, 8, 9

Private Collections
  Figures 10a, g, 11a, b, h, i, k
  Plates 8b, c, 9a, b, c, 10a, c, 12a, b, c, d, 13c, 15c, d

*Photo Credits*
  Figure 4      V. Goloubew
  Figure 2      Government of Indonesia

All other photographs are by the author

# Introduction

IN Central Java, at Surakarta, in the old sultans' palace is an iron meteorite. There, in a garden by a pool under two mango trees, on the floor of a small, raised pavilion, lies the brownish lump known as the Prambanan meteor (Plate 1).

The meteorite, resembling a large, pitted rock about the breadth of a man's arm, was brought to the *kraton* in the year 1797. It had fallen some fifty years earlier at an ancient temple site twenty-seven miles from Surakarta, then the seat of government. The meteorite is regarded as holy; a few little pots of withering flowers testify to this. No one may touch it now; it is sacred, in a place of rest, and offerings of fruit and flowers are made to it.

It is part of a larger mass which signalled its violent arrival by bursting into two pieces at the end of its fiery journey near the temples of Prambanan some 200 years ago. One of the pieces, the smaller chunk, was brought to the *kraton* (palace) in 1784. There, the palace *empu*, master swordsmiths, forged a few weapons which they believed would possess magic or talismanic properties because of the celestial origin of the iron that was used. Some of these weapons, in dagger form known as 'kris', are still to be found in various museums. Others, long lost to record, are no doubt in private hands, owned by unsuspecting collectors.

There are other accounts of weapons being made from meteor iron, but none as revealing and verifiable as the history of the Prambanan meteor falls. In the study of the kris, a great part of which is concerned with magic and mysticism on one hand, and iron and metallurgy on the other, the Prambanan meteor seems to represent perfectly the combination of properties encountered in this unusual weapon.

There is an abundance of old literature concerning the kris written in English over the past two centuries, with ample counterparts in other languages. The scholarly collector soon discovers that the kris is no ordinary sword. Of course, it is a weapon with a blade of steel but was only rarely used in battle. Because of its lightness and an inherent weakness at the tang, the kris was seldom used in aggressive combat and certainly was not adequate in defence against heavier weapons.

Therefore, except for a few detailed descriptions by dedicated technical specialists devoted to the metallurgy of the blade, most writings on the kris bear on the magical and supernatural aspects of the weapon. Important sub-topics are the symbolism of the damascene designs forged into the blades; the talismanic virtue of these designs; deity and mythform derivations in the numerous styles of the hilt; traditional uses of the kris in ceremony and ritual, and the role of the kris in drama, particularly in plays of mythological origins. Almost never will one find writings on the proper use of the weapon in defence or attack.

The sum of all of this is that the kris, once widely worn as a deterrent to hostility, has become increasingly a cultural talisman. It is used in a symbolic and ritualistic way, thus assuring the wearer of proper status as a Malay, and in Java particularly, as a symbol of Javanese manhood. Thus, among all weapons the kris is unique in that its principal function has long been that of cultural association rather than of an extension of the hand for doing harm to others.

# I

# The Kris and Its Origins

THE kris is the distinctive weapon of Malaysia and Indonesia. These countries form the geographical and cultural area once referred to as the Malay world. The kris is found in a variety of forms ranging from northern Sumatra and Malaysia to far-distant Mindanao in the Philippines (see map, endpapers). All of the forms show decided similarities which unite krises into a single, easily recognized family.

Typically the kris is an elongated dagger (Malay, *keris*, 'dagger') or short sword of slender proportions with a blade of rough texture sharpened on both edges. The base of the blade at the hilt always widens at one side in an appearance suggestive of a modified sword-catching arrangement. This part is called the *ganja*, and it is the sudden widening on one side only that unites all krises into a common family (Figures 1, 6). The kris is seldom very sharp; this combined with its light weight indicates that it evolved as a thrusting weapon for personal defence.

The blade may be sinuous or straight and is often damascened with beautiful patterns forged into the steel. The wavy or serpentine blade is regarded as the classic kris form, but it is probably pre-dated by the straight blade form. Straight blades are plentiful in collections; they may be found in an approximate ratio of two straight blades to three wavy blades.

There are many theories as to the origin of the kris. One school predominantly Western, holds that the weapon evolved in Central Java prior to the fourteenth century from Hindu beginnings. Firm evidence that the kris existed in that era was first reported by Raffles (1817) after visiting the ruins of the Hindu temple at Sukuh, twenty-six miles east of Surakarta.

Raffles, a brilliant scholar and tireless observer, provides a

3

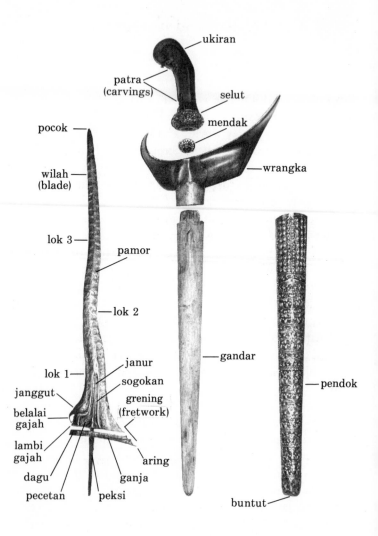

Figure 1. The Parts of a Kris.

4

Figure 2. Candi Sukuh forge scene, *c.* 1361.

sketch of Vishnu, one of the principal Hindu gods, holding a kris while straddling his mount, the bird-god Garuda. Then he provides a sketch and an excellent description of what has since become known as the Candi[1] Sukuh forge scene. The forge scene is a sculptured stone triptych depicting the manufacture of what surely must be kris blades (Figure 2).

The triptych is indeed interesting. The left panel clearly shows the forging of kris blades by an *empu* god, while the right panel shows another figure operating a pair of cylindrical bellows of the type well known to Malay smiths. The left figure has been identified as Bima, a lesser Hindu god. Bima was brother to Arjuna, who was an ally of and brother-in-law to Krishna. Both were warriors and armourers, Bima having the greater physical strength and stronger character. No doubt the figure operating the bellows is Arjuna.

---

[1] *Candi* (Malay—pronounced 'chundy') means temple.

5

The central panel, which at first glance seems irrelevant to the scene, is a depiction of Ganesa, the elephant god and the god of good beginnings who ensures success to the worthy in any new undertaking. At such times offerings are properly made to Ganesa; thus artisans and smiths offer their tools for blessing. In turn Ganesa seems to be providing an animal for sacrifice—a practice which is prevalent in India today.

Raffles, interpreting these inscriptions with the aid of scholars he employed in his work, established the date AD 1361 for the Candi Sukuh complex. No positive earlier evidence of the kris has yet been offered. So the weapon in a form that we recognize as a kris is at least 600 years old according to the evidence of the Candi Sukuh carvings. Groneman, in his writings (1910) provides a photograph of a similar forge scene, showing vertical bellows still in use in Java at the time of his research (Figure 3).

Figure 3. Groneman's forge scene, c. 1910. Note the similar vertical cylindrical bellows at the right of each scene.

Just fifty miles west of Surakarta lies the huge Buddhist temple of Borobudur. It is an enormous stepped pyramid of eight levels, each of which provides a continuous terrace around the perimeter of the structure. The walls of the lower four levels contain more than half a mile of bas-relief carvings in stone showing incidents in the life of Buddha and of his bodhisattvas. The temple, of South Indian design, was completed in the ninth century AD. Because of the vast numbers of portrayals in stone of every aspect of the human condition the scenes revealed in the carvings have become of inestimable value to researchers. There are numerous scenes showing the use or carrying of weapons of various types.

However, despite 165 years of recorded scrutiny, no weapon, of the many portrayed, has yet been positively identified as an early kris. Therefore it would seem that the kris did not exist in the ninth century but did exist in the middle of the fourteenth century.

Javanese legends variously place the origin of the kris much earlier, a little before, and at about the same time as the Candi Sukuh evidence. This uncertainty is not unlike legends in general, but it seems wise to take heed of any information, nebulous as it may be, which might prove a possible link to verifiable evidence.

Ostmeier, a Dutchman in government service, examined six Javanese manuscripts which recorded the work of *empu* and the monarchs who ordered their works. He concluded that the contents of the different manuscripts were fairly consistent in respect to the names of the monarchs and *empu* and the chronology of kris manufacture. However, he found that other information in them varied widely from one to another, and all had to be discredited because of its uncertainty.

According to Ostmeier's readings, the first krises were manufactured between the years 152 and 210 of the Javanese calendar (AD 230–88). These were straight blade types, with the first sinuous blade being recorded in the Javanese year 251 (AD 329). His account goes on to describe and name no less than fifty-one krises, the names of the reigning monarchs and their *empu*, all recorded up to AD 1607.

A more accepted Javanese account attributes the introduction of the kris to Panji, a hero-prince in story and drama who lived *c.* AD 920. Panji, whose origins are uncertain, was supposed to have introduced the kris, the *gamelan* orchestra and the *wayang* drama form to the 'Easterly Islands' (i.e. from South India?).

Another legend reveals that an ancient Hindu prince, Sakutram, was born with a *keris pasopati*, a straight blade form, at his side—not a likely occurrence. It is interesting to find, however, that Rice (1978) defines *pasopati* as one of the aspects of the Hindu god, Shiva. This provides another tantalizing link with the Hindu origin theory of the kris.

Finally, a more popular legend tells of an Inakarta Pati, King of Janggala in East Java, who early in the fourteenth century introduced the first kris. Perhaps this is also myth, but it should be noted that there is no archaeological evidence to support the existence of the kris prior to that time.

In addition, there are some more pragmatic views as to the origin of the kris. These theories deal with the probable origin and evolution of kris-like daggers in South-East Asia based on harder evidence than mere mythology. Gardner (1936) offers his belief that the metal kris evolved from the sharp, barbed dorsal spine of a sting-ray,[1] a fish common to Malay waters. Gardner refers to findings of this type of primitive weapon in the 'Dutch East Indies' at Stone Age sites five or six days journey from the sea.

In his work on this theory, Gardner found that by wrapping the base of a sting from a ray in cloth or bark, thus providing a hilt, he could well duplicate the earliest all-metal kris. The

[1] Malay, *ikan pari*, or ray fish.

one-piece all-metal kris of which numerous examples exist is thought to have originated in the fourteenth century. It is termed *keris majapahit* after its supposed introduction during that dynastic period to Java and the neighbouring islands (Figure 5).

Some small evidence exists for the idea that the Majapahit kris evolved from an Annamite type of dagger (Figure 4). Many bronze and some iron artefacts dating from the third century BC have been unearthed near Dong-Son, a village eighty-five miles south of Hanoi. The great diversity of the artefacts found in the grave-sites at Dong-Son has caused the area to be regarded as the focal point of the Bronze Age in Mainland South-East Asia and Indonesia with far-reaching and permanent influence on the art of the area. Nevertheless it does not seem likely that a Dong-Son dagger was ancestor to the kris, as no weapon of that type has yet been discovered in Indonesia that can be dated less than 1500

Figure 4. A Dong-Son Dagger, *c.* 300 BC. An old photograph with diagrammatic views of a bronze dagger in the Musée de Hanoi.

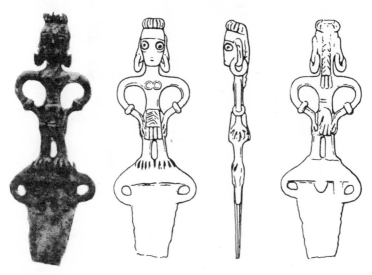

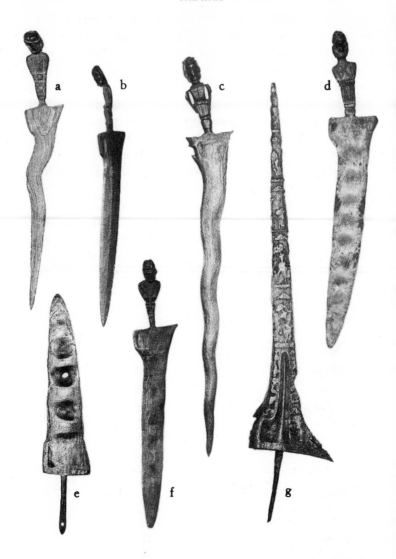

Figure 5. Early Krises and Blades. (a), (b), (c) Early *keris majapahit*; (d), (f) *keris majapahit picit*; (e) *keris buda*; (g) an early, fully evolved kris with engraved *wayang* figures.

years later. Surely some examples would have appeared in that long period if the kris form had existed then.

Thus the origins of the well-known Majapahit kris are still elusive. This kris form is generally regarded as the oldest one that can be verified, but here, too, there are pitfalls. There also exists a rare type known as *keris buda* (Buddha) (Figure 5) a kris thought to be older than *keris majapahit*, although this cannot be verified. This type usually takes the form of a rough, short and wide blade. It has a squared tang, rather than the bent-over human figure which always forms the hilt of the Majapahit kris.

All in all, the origin of the kris is a mystery that remains unsolved. Whether of divine or Indian origin, patterned after sharp, organic objects, descendant from distant cultures or confounded by unreliable manuscripts, these are questions which go unanswered. Now, with increasing attention being given to the subject, perhaps the mystery will finally be resolved.

# 2

# The Magic and the Power
# of the Kris

THE history of the kris abounds with stories of its magic powers. Old legends, and indeed some modern tales, grip the imagination of the reader with bizarre and fascinating accounts of this mysterious weapon.

Many stories are told of krises that slew by the mere act of being pointed at the victim. There is much superstitious lore, and the Malays in particular believed in a form of magic called *tuju*. With appropriate incantations, and the deliberate pointing of a finger, human bone or kris at a person, could bring bad luck or disaster upon him. A *keris bertuah* (fortunate or lucky kris) was especially powerful in this regard. With such a kris a man could be done in simply by stabbing his footprints. Illness and death always followed.

Some of the old magic krises were credited with having strong wills, an animus, of their own. One kris kept on display in the museum at Taiping in Malaysia would thirst for blood, sneak away after dark, kill someone, wash and wipe itself and return to its showcase in secret. Another kris, a *keris pusaka* (heirloom kris) was especially bad-tempered. It left its sheath and the *kraton* every night to search out a victim and draw blood. The ruler of the *kraton* ordered the kris destroyed when its bad temper and evil activities were reported by three other krises. The evil kris was smashed to grit in a mortar; its fine particles are supposed to have risen to the sky on that particularly starry night.

Stories are told of krises that rattled in their sheaths to warn of danger and of krises that murmured approving sounds when drawn, disapproving when sheathed. A well-educated Javanese translator known to the author swears that his brother has a kris that will stand on its tip on command. One kris of Mataram (*c.* 1600) was supposedly made of iron originating from nine different places and from nine different objects, the names of which all started with the letter P. All this ironware had been acquired by theft. The kris was forged by beating with a hammer just one blow every Friday. Of course, it took a long time to complete but once finished it possessed magic properties. Trees withered when touched by it, and any animal coming close to its hiding place died on the spot. Ostmeier tells of a kris, which he apparently inspected, that was completed after being worked at the forge for seventeen years at the rate of two minutes per day. He also met an *empu* who had been working on another kris for thirteen years. The *empu* revealed a dream in which he was to start a new kris on the birth of a son and forge it only for as long as the crowing of the roosters each day. He believed that if he followed the dream faithfully, his son would, because of this magic kris, rise to a high position in the government.

A fifteenth century hero of Malacca, Hang Tuah, who is said to have introduced the kris into the country, owned a very loyal specimen. It was special in that it was made of twenty types of iron. Hang Tuah asserted that if he were menaced, the kris would leap out of its sheath, fly through the air and attack his assailant by itself.

In another tale, a Muslim general used a specially potent *keris pusaka* against some Javanese soldiers. When pointed at the Javanese, a swarm of angry hornets emerged from its tip. The same general had in his arsenal a coat of chain-mail from which a horde of frantic rats could be released in the heat of battle.

In the *Pararaton*, an old Javanese chronicle, the story is told of Ken Arok, a prince of divine birth who meets the wife of a local governor. As she alights from a carriage her gown is caught up in it, revealing her thighs. Ken Arok sees that 'her lap radiates a blaze . . . her feminine organ glows like fire'. He becomes wild with desire and plots to kill her husband with a specially prepared kris crafted by a local *empu* named Gandring. After five months the kris is still not ready. Ken Arok, beside himself with impatience and rage, attacks the *empu*. The *empu* retaliates by laying a curse on Ken Arok, according to which his children and his children's children, are all to die by that same kris. Eventually the curse takes effect, and Ken Arok is stabbed to death in the back by the infamous weapon.

Many stories are told of kris blades formed while red-hot from the pressure of the *empu*'s fingers or thumbs. Such daggers are called *keris pichit*; they have short, wide and thin blades with four or five thumb-like impressions and corresponding swells on the other side. This type of kris may be as old as *keris majapahit*. One legend attributes this finger-shaping ability to a Bugis sovereign of the Celebes (Sulawesi). The prince, born, it is said of a supernatural being, introduced the manufacture of krises to his land by shaping the hot iron with his fingers. In Solo (Surakarta) there once lived a female *empu* named Sounbrou who is said to have forged a *keris betok* (fish-like) by simply shaping the hot blade with her bare fingers.

Some Malays believed that the *keris majapahit* had a sexual identity—that a large kris was male, a small kris female. One legend avers that a *keris majapahit* made by a certain *empu*, was made red-hot, then tempered by being drawn between his armpit and finally thrust into a tub of water. To show equal skill, a female *empu* of the same village, fashioned a smaller, female kris, by drawing the red-hot blade between the lips of her vulva and thrusting it into the tempering water.

Perhaps the oddest power that is attributed to kris magic is the ability to divert and redirect flames from a burning structure. Flames will follow the tip of such a kris but the flames will not be affected if the fire is set deliberately to test the kris. The dual powers of *tuju* and fire-directing are supposed to be contained in the soul of *keris majapahit*. The story is told of a Malay whose house caught fire. A friend brought out a special kris and, although 'sparks flew all around', the flames were diverted. When asked why he did not save the other houses nearby, the Malay replied, 'They were not my houses'. There is no record of the type of kris used in this incident.

A magic kris also had power with water. Skeat, surely the master of Malay folklore, writing in 1900 provides a detailed account of an approved method to extract water from a kris:

> The *Pawang* (magician) works with any kris. He holds it point downward and recites an incantation—the gist of it being that he is master of the iron and it must obey him. After gently rubbing and squeezing the blade with his thumb and two fingers, water begins to drip from the point. Gradually it becomes a steady trickle—enough to fill a cup.

Unfortunately, however, something is lost in the process, for 'The kris blade no longer has good temper and the kris is without value'.

A number of accounts exist which explain how to enlarge the deadly powers of the kris. Jasper and Pirngadie, writing in Dutch in 1930, have preserved much of this lore. Islanders of Madura, they say, dip the kris blade in the brains or viscera of scorpions and snakes to make the weapon more deadly. Furthermore, in Java a treatment known as *tjatjap* consists of bringing the blade of the kris into contact with the brains or guts of a snake. All this makes the kris more deadly and its value is enhanced with each person it slays. A kris that had been used in many killings was often regarded as sacred.

In kris lore there are many legends which one may think quaint and archaic—but superstition does not die easily. As recently as 1983 more lore was added to the reputation of the kris for its magic powers when J. Kronholz, a Western journalist, reported an interview with a number of *empu* still practising their trade in the Yogyakarta area. The article contains many surprises.

One *empu* maintained that a magic kris will befuddle a robber. 'He approaches the house, he is overwhelmed, he cannot go in.' He went on, 'A kris can foil a murderer, he can't bend his trigger finger... of course, a kris can extinguish fires, hold back flood waters or divert volcano flows.' Another *empu* was quoted as saying, 'When the invisible Queen of the South Seas holds court on the Javanese seashore the krises come out of their sheaths and fly down to the beach.' A craftsman connected to the *kraton* at Surakarta claimed, 'They (the krises) fly all around the palace but they are no problem—mostly it's the magic spears that we have trouble with.'

Kronholz continues to quote the *empu*: 'It is not easy to make magic swords. I must ask God for the magic—the Moslem God, the Catholic God, the one God for all the people.' Further, 'A kris has to fit, a lowly man with the arrogance to buy a kris made for a general will suffer misfortune... I might become sick if I use a kris too strong for me... in business everything might go wrong.'

For a reasonable price one *empu* offers a kris with three-fold magic. 'It will prevent your house from burning down, it will protect you from being killed by a gun and it will divert floodwaters.'

From all of this it is apparent that the cult of the magic kris is very much alive today in Java, which is after all, a civilized part of the world.

# 3

# The Kris as Cultural Talisman

FOR the past hundred years, perhaps for as little as forty years in some parts of the Malay world, the kris has ceased to be worn for personal protection. Because of the presence of the Dutch and English in South-East Asia from the seventeenth century onwards, the need or right to carry a weapon gradually fell into abeyance. The Western colonizers gradually imposed their own laws and controls upon native society.

Throughout this process the kris has been retained in ceremonial as a symbol of the heritage it represents. It is used throughout the Malay world on every sort of grand occasion, its presence usually denoting a particularly important affair. The history of its use in ceremonial and ritual is as old as the kris itself (Plate 16). Literature is full of wondrous accounts that impress upon the reader the profound meaning of the kris in Malaysian and Indonesian culture. Indeed, one author may have spoken for the whole region when he wrote, 'Java without the kris would not be Java'.

Holstein, in his masterpiece in French (1931), has a particular flair for this kind of tale. He ferrets out the best of all the old writings from his vast reference library on weaponry. He explains that the kris held first rank among the weapons used by the Malays; it was the supreme national weapon to which divine origin was attributed. A Malay man without a kris was despised; if he were not a serf he always carried a kris, and would be ashamed to leave his house without it. Certainly this idea is embodied in an old Javanese aphorism, recently translated into modern Javanese by the scholarly Solyums (1978), that five things are most sacred to the Javanese man—*wisma, wanita, kukila, turongga, curiga*—his home, his wife, his birds, his horse and his weapon (a kris, of course).

Other accounts relate that many Malays of rank did not address one another unless accompanied by their krises; that a Malay 'never moved' without his kris; when he bathed it was with him and also when he slept. Many men raised the kris to their foreheads each time it was drawn as a sign of respect to the spirit of the kris. When a merchant arrived in Aceh (North Sumatra) he could not unload his goods until the head of customs had initiated the required ceremony by raising his kris (with hilt of gold) to the head of the merchant. Most of the inhabitants of Macassar, in southern Celebes (Sulawesi) did not touch their krises without first pronouncing sacred words. Raffles once proposed to limit the wearing of krises to royalty and officials, but was dissuaded by a local ruler who explained, most frankly, that the Malay without his kris would feel naked.

Many accounts tell of oaths and obeisance done, using the kris as the ritual component. The taking of an oath (*bersumpah*) was a serious matter when associated with certain holy objects. A *keramat* is a kind of shrine, sometimes a grave. For a Malay it was unthinkable to violate an oath taken in such a place. Another term, *besi kawi* (ancient iron) designated the next most sacrosanct component that could be used in ritual oath-taking. The term was made use of by the Sumatrans to formulate a most ugly curse, saying essentially, 'May you be struck down by the poison of *kawi*'.

The most common procedure for oath-taking consisted of sprinkling lime juice on the blade of the kris. The citric acid attacked the blade, forming a rusty, acidic deposit. Mixed with water, this bitter potion left a stain on the lips of one who sipped it. The stain was symbolic of the stigma that would revert to him should he fail to keep his oath.

In Lampong (South Sumatra) oaths were taken by dipping the point of the kris in water, catching the run-off on the tongue and swearing to accept punishment if the oath were broken. In Sumatra generally, when an oath of fidelity to a local ruler was to be made, an old rusty kris or one which had some extraordinary property attributed to it was plunged into water and given to the oath-taker. He slowly drank the water as he pronounced a sacred formula, the words, in this case, being '*Jika aku belut, aku dimakan keris*', meaning, 'If I turn traitor, may I be consumed by this kris'.

The kris is frequently found today at Malaysian and Indonesian wedding ceremonies. It is a traditional part of the groom's costume and completes his image of acceptability in the eyes of the bride and her family. The kris worn by the groom is a gift from his new father-in-law or, in his absence, from the brother of the bride (Plate 2).

There is a rich and colourful history to this ceremony. Raffles again provides us with some of the earliest information. Beside an excellent description of the pre-nuptial proceedings, noting in process a surprising similarity to biblical and Roman rites, he reports in great detail on all aspects of the ceremony.

He notes that in Malay custom the kris is accepted as a substitute for the groom. Should any circumstance prevent the bridegroom from being present on the day selected, the bride might be married to the groom's kris. This seemed to be a special privilege enjoyed by those of higher rank when marrying lower-status women, as the practice was infrequent in first marriages of commoners. A local chief could force a daughter of a commoner to become attached to his house. This practice met with such resentment that the demanding chief often ordered the girl to be married to his kris rather than to himself.

The Malay words *panjat angkara* (entry by violence) signify forced entry into a house for the purpose of abducting a girl whose family have already refused the intruder's previous offers of marriage. Custom allowed such conduct if prescribed rules were obeyed: The man, armed with his kris, risks injury from the girl's family but he must not retaliate. The family in turn, must, privately at least, take into consideration the intruder's reputation, his friends, and his family status. If they, (the girl's family) acquiesce, the suitor must be prepared to pay double the usual bride-price and a fine for trespassing according to his means. One story is told of an exorbitant trespass fine being levied, the sum going to the girl's other lover, the new suitor's disappointed rival. Sometimes the girl's relatives would not yield; then the rejected swain, retreating hastily, suffered considerable embarrassment to himself in the village.

In another account, a maddened lover forced his way into the girl's house, seized her by her long hair and threatened to kill her with his kris. Of course he did not go as far as that, but he defied everyone for three days and nights, finally being tricked with some drugged food given to him by the girl's family. The girl, now released, was taken away and a few days later, was married to another suitor. The end of the story is tragic. Within a few months the rejected suitor, brooding over his loss, ran *amok*.[1] In his anguish he killed the rival husband with his kris and wounded the former object of his love.

The term *panjat adat* denotes a more pacific way of pressing for a bride when the girl's family is adamant. In this case the kris is used merely as a symbol of forced entry. The suitor sends his kris to the girl's home with a message that he is prepared to meet the bride-price and gift requirements, doubled according to tradition, and further, is willing to meet any other demands. The kris may be returned as a symbol of continued refusal, but, if so, the bride's family must pay the suitor an agreed-upon rejection price.

The bride-price usually consisted of a sum of money, often quite large, and of gifts lesser in value. In Sumatra, however, a custom existed of substituting a fine kris—one with a sheath and fittings of gold or silver—for the money. Generally, a

---

[1] A term denoting an uncontrollable frenzy, a form of violence peculiar to Malay society.

commoner had to be careful not to display a kris excessively adorned, out of keeping with a man of his status.

The use of gold in regalia was widespread throughout the Malay world, as it has been in royal affairs everywhere. Usually a hilt of gold on a fine kris denoted royalty or, at least, connection to the court. A number of Malay terms may be applied to gold-mounted krises—*keris gayang* (gold kris); *keris gabus* (gold sheath); *keris hulu kenchana* (gold hilt), etc. (Plates 6 and 7). A red stain from the tamarind fruit was often used to impart a rich background colour to the goldwork. Sometimes gold was combined with copper to produce the alloy *suasa*; it can be recognized by the handsome pink tint it gives to the copper. The term usually applied to a kris of antiquity and importance was *keris pusaka*, an heirloom kris, one that had special ritual significance to the bearer and his followers.

A fine kris with hilt and scabbard of gold was given to the British king, James I, in 1613 by the Sultan of Aceh (North Sumatra). It was of the type being crafted at that time in Menangkabau. This area was the origin of much fine gold work using a detailed filigree style and advanced soldering techniques. Hill (1956) writes that on great occasions the *Susuhanan* (supreme overlord) of Mataram, the east Javanese empire, displayed the royal kris hung on a belt which with its sheath was a blaze of diamonds. Only the officials of this court were allowed to display hilts of gold on their krises. As recently as 1901 in the Malaysian state of Negeri Sembilan it was decreed that the wearing of a kris with hilt and scabbard of gold was a special privilege reserved for members of the royal house.

The Malacca Code, probably instituted by Sultan Muhammad Shah in 1415, prescribed strict procedures for the wearing of a kris. A person not part of the palace retinue was prohibited from wearing a *keris hulu kenchana*, one with a gold hilt, suffering confiscation of the weapon if he disregarded the Code.

To the Malays, gold was more than precious; it was believed

to be the holy gift of a *dewa* or god and its retrieval from the beaches of Sumatra, or the mines of the Malay Peninsula was done with preparations mindful of the god's sensitivity to intrusion. Thus the use of gold was widely restricted by royalty on grounds of superstition as well as for the purpose of enhancing their own status by their special right to use it.

Although some of the ceremonial, associated with the kris has diminished, the kris remains firmly a part of *wayang* (drama) performances. In the Malay *wayang* are re-enacted tales from the great Hindu epic poems, the *Ramayana* and the *Mahabharata*. This kind of entertainment was once widespread in Malaysia and is still frequent in Indonesia in the form of shadow plays, puppet shows and human performances (Plates 4 and 5). The kris appears and reappears, sometimes necessary to the plot, sometimes simply as part of the costuming. The dance repertoire throughout the entire area also includes krises in story or costume, the dances generally being re-enactments of some epic tale. Balinese and Javanese dances in particular include the mighty, mystical kris (Plates 3 and 4). All-night performances in villages, with the audience seated on the ground, are still frequent; but increasingly, in order to cater for tourists, the plays have become short, carefully-staged productions supported with an elaborate *gamelan* orchestra. In this way some of the beauty of the *wayang* is imparted to many foreigners, who because of limitations of time could not otherwise have enjoyed it.

# 4
# The Deadly Kris

FOR all the magic, and mysticism and ritual associated with the kris, it was, for the first few hundred years of its existence, primarily a weapon of defence and sudden assault. Literature abounds with accounts of its use in assassinations and executions, intrigues, rivalry and sneak attacks. Indeed, at one time and in some areas it was considered a despicable weapon, fit only for brigands, a weapon of treachery and with poisonous qualities at that. The very smallness of the weapon, fitted as it was with a bent-over or pistol-like grip, made it a perfect stabbing instrument. It was easy to make a straight-line thrust to the belly or kidney of a victim while the elbow was bent. This made it effective in a confined space and no doubt contributed to its reputation as a weapon of ill repute.

Nor did its association with poisons help its image. For Europeans, at least, the great sin of the kris was that it poisoned its victim. How this conjecture came about is uncertain, for there are no accounts, sketchy or detailed, which tell of anyone being poisoned by a kris. Despite this, an example is given of a kris in Macassar which was poisonous and which did poison everyone who touched it—except its owner! Gardner thought the idea of a venomous kris must have come from its association with the sting-ray whose body contains a gland of poison. When the fish's sting is removed, some of its barbs remain, the wound festers and death often follows. Gardner's idea seems plausible, as the ray's sting has been reported in use in North Malaya as late as 1936. However, writers on Malay subjects dispense with the idea of poisonous kris blades, having seen none in their time.

There is general agreement that the treatment of kris blades to accentuate the *pamor*, the damascene-like patterns forged into the blade, does create residues which may be harmful if ingested or allowed to enter the blood stream. Given that the solutions created by citric acids and arsenic compounds on steel are noxious, there is no evidence that these solutions so penetrate the interstices of the blade *pamor* that the wound becomes fatal. Of course the wound, irritated and inflamed by chemical action, is harder to heal, but it is not surely fatal as it might be if true poison were used. Although there are accounts of arrow-heads, small daggers, spears and blow-pipe darts being prepared with poisons, the results expected were not always obtained. The poisons, generally herbal, dry out and deteriorate quickly, often proving to be an unreliable factor in an armed assault.

It is not unlikely that some of the idea of a poisonous kris derived from the association of the blade with a Naga—the Sanskrit term for snake. Many old descriptions of the blade liken it to a snake in motion—a serpentine blade; or, a snake at rest—a straight blade. Rare and especially valued is a *keris naga*—one with the carved likeness of a snake's body running the length of its blade and terminating in a snake or dragon's head near the *ganja* (Plate 13c). The *keris majapahit* was sometimes regarded as poisonous. The poison was thought to be part of the old iron—and perhaps six hundred years of rust was poisonous in itself. With such a kris, a mere puncture to the depth of the white of a fingernail was said to be fatal.

Despite its reputation for evil-doing, the kris was used extensively for necessary lethal acts—acts in most cases sanc-tioned by some governing authority. According to Wallace, the laws in force on the island of Lombok were very strict at the time of his visit. Theft was punished by being 'krissed' and a stranger found in a house after dark might be stabbed with a kris, his body dragged out and 'no questions asked'. Similar laws are related by Cool, who visited the island of Bali. Adultery, incest, and treason were punishable by being krissed, as were also murders and thefts committed during the night. A milder form of punishment might consist of cutting out the tongue of the accused. On this island, which follows the Hindu faith and traditions, a surviving wife would sacrifice herself on her husband's funeral pyre. The custom, patterned after the Hindu *suttee*, was often resisted by Balinese women who preferred being krissed, sometimes administering the fatal blow themselves.

The story goes of an English trader who had a Balinese woman living with him—a not unacceptable arrangement according to Balinese custom at that time. When it was learned that she had encouraged a slight favour—a festival flower—from another man, the local Raja ordered her to be krissed. The Englishman intervened in her behalf and the matter was ostensibly dropped. However, a few weeks later a messenger came to the girl's door saying, 'The Raja sends you this', and stabbed her to the heart with a kris.

The manner of formal execution is well recorded: A *keris panjang*, one having a narrow straight blade, eighteen or more inches in length, was used. The condemned was seated, or sometimes knelt, his arms held by guards on either side. The executioner stood behind, or sometimes facing, holding the kris vertically. The point rested on a wad of cotton which had been placed on the victim's shoulder, near the neck just behind the collar-bone. When the signal was given, often by the Raja himself, but in his absence by the authority of his gold-sheathed kris, the blade was driven downward through the heart of the condemned. A quick thrust of ten to twelve inches penetrated the entire heart; death was fast and merciful. As the blade was withdrawn, it was wiped clean on the cotton pad.

Because it was bloodless, this method of execution was preferred over the use of a broad sword to decapitate the condemned—a style also practised. In some remote parts of the Malay world a similar procedure using the heavier blade of a spear was known.

Several instances are told of criminals being exposed to combat with tigers as a form of execution. This barbarous practice was observed as late 1807 in Central Java during the reign of the *Susuhanan* of Yogyakarta who was deposed by the British in 1812. On one occasion two criminals, confined in a large cage built for the purpose, were each given a kris with the tip broken off. A tiger was let into the cage; one criminal was soon mauled to death. However, the remaining victim was able to avoid serious injury over a period of two hours, by repeatedly attacking and cutting the tiger about the head, eyes and ears. He finally succeeded in killing the beast, only to have a leopard released into the cage. He was able to destroy this animal as well. The man's captors, astonished and impressed with his remarkable performance, set him free and indeed elevated him to a minor post in the *kraton*.

Early in the seventeenth century the English and the Dutch each established their own 'East India Companies' for the purpose of trade in the islands of the Malay Archipelago. Dutch naval strength gradually forced the Portuguese to withdraw from their many outposts in the region. The English, anxious to participate in local trade, nevertheless, fell far behind in the race to get to the 'Spice Islands', and sought energetically to obtain trading privileges in key locations. Spices, particularly pepper and cloves, were in great demand throughout Europe to assure supplies of palatable meat. Spices masked the flavour of the heavily salted meat which was often dreary fare. In 1603 the English shipped home a million pounds of pepper from Sumatra alone.

Judging from old writings it is evident that there was mutual dislike and rivalry between the Dutch and English in the settlements they often shared together. Henry Middleton, in command of the second expedition of the English East India Company to the region, reports extensively on native affairs in a thorough account of this journey. Written in 1605, it is one of the earliest records to contain detail regarding the use of the kris throughout the islands. Some of the stories are grisly reminders of the medieval attitudes still prevalent among Westerners in the treatment of prisoners. Scott, one of the captains on the voyage, tells of a quarrel between the English and Dutch over a mulatto man-servant belonging to the English group. The mulatto had killed with his 'cryse' a Dutch official who had insulted him. Then he killed a shipmate who had witnessed the deed and killed yet another, an unfortunate Javanese who happened on the scene.

The Dutch were incensed at the killing of one of their countrymen and the local Raja was equally angered at the killing of one of his subjects. They demanded compensation for the murders in the form of torture and mutilation for the killer. The demand was granted but Scott refused to turn over his man to the Dutch authorities, insisting on the English right to punish one of their own miscreants. Finally, Scott was reduced to arguing with the Dutch over the form of the execution itself. The Dutch arrived with a firing-squad on the morning of the execution but Scott had already made prior arrangements with a hired *pelebaya* (executioner) used by the Javanese Raja in such matters. The prisoner was dispatched quickly with Scott's own kris, thus ending the affair to everyone's satisfaction.

\*     \*     \*

A dissertation on the deadliness of the kris is hardly complete without some discussion of the Malay behaviour known as running *amok*. Webster's Dictionary defines it succinctly as follows:

amuck, amok 1. a Malay running wild in a murderous frenzy and attacking everyone he meets. 2. a nervous malady or seizure peculiar to the Malays, resulting in a murderous frenzy.

In Marsden's Dictionary is given:

*amuk* engaging furiously in battle; attacking with desperate resolution; rushing, in a state of frenzy, to the commission of indiscriminate murder; running amuck.

The term was first used in the Portuguese form *amouco*, *amuco*, by Barbosa (1514) who said (in translation): 'There are some of them (the Javanese) who go out into the streets and kill as many as they meet, these are called Amuco.'

The sheer drama of an ordinary and peaceful citizen suddenly running wild in a murderous frenzy captures the imagination of all of us. Although *amok* is the Malay style of such behaviour, similar violent behaviour, for different psychological reasons, is well known both in primitive and modern societies. One source regards *amok* as a form of suicide that has been conventionalized in Malay society. It is caused by a desperation due to romantic or domestic difficulties, or by brooding on some aspect of personal misfortune. When *amok* is considered by modern psychologists, it is put into categories with similar behaviour patterns. *Amok* belongs to a group of mental disorders labelled culture-bound disorders because their unusual symptoms are determined by cultural or societal factors. One psychologist (Yap, 1974) divides these aberrant forms of behaviour into reactions of fear, of rage and of hysteria. He calls *amok* a rage reaction. Another investigator (Kiev, 1972) fits *amok* into one of six classifications—anxious, obsessional, hysterical, phobic, depressive, and dissociative. According to him *amok* is a dissociative type of mental disorder. Yap's rage category satisfies better the traditional idea of *amok*, which sometimes involves more than one person. Kiev's dissociative category does not seem compatible with the generally accepted causes of *amok* or the fact of a group of people who have run *amok*.

The *keris* and *amok* go hand in hand. Both are distinctly and inseparably Malay, and most accounts of *amok* behaviour involve a lethal kris. In the old literature there are many stories of this excited form of behaviour but none as dramatically descriptive as a paragraph penned by Wallace (1869). The full flavour of Wallace's splendid writing is evident in this account:

Macassar is the most celebrated place in the East for "running a muck". There are said to be one or two a month on the average, and five, ten, or twenty persons are sometimes killed or wounded at one of them. It is the national and therefore the honourable mode of committing suicide among the natives of Celebes, and is the fashionable way of escaping from their difficulties. A Roman fell upon his sword, a Japanese rips up his stomach, and an Englishman blows out his brains with a pistol. The Bugis mode has many advantages to one suicidally inclined. A man thinks himself wronged by society—he is in debt and cannot pay—he is taken for a slave or has gambled away his wife or child into slavery—he sees no way of recovering what he has lost, and becomes desperate. He will not put up with such cruel wrongs, but will be revenged on mankind and die like a hero. He grasps his kris-handle, and the next moment draws out the weapon and stabs a man to the heart. He runs on, with the bloody kris in his hand, stabbing at every one he meets. "Amok! Amok!" then resounds through the streets. Spears, krisses, knives and guns are brought out against him. He rushes madly forward, kills all he can—men, women, and children—and dies overwhelmed by numbers amid all the excitement of a battle. And what that excitement is those who have been in one best know, but all who have ever given way to violent passions, or even indulged in violent and exciting exercises, may form a very good idea. It is a delirious intoxication, a temporary madness that absorbs every thought and every energy. And can we wonder at the kris-bearing, untaught, brooding Malay preferring such a death, looked upon as almost honourable, to the cold-blooded details of suicide, if he wishes to escape from overwhelming troubles, or the merciless clutches of the hangman and the disgrace of a public execution, when he has taken the law into his own hands, and too hastily revenged himself upon his enemy? In either case he chooses rather to "amok".

# 5
# The Kris and Its Blade

THE preceding chapters have dealt with the mysticism and cultural value of the kris. Certainly these unique aspects impart to the kris some of the magic of the Tibetan ghost-dagger (phurbu) and some of the national pride represented in a samurai long-sword (katana). Now it is time to describe the physical body of the kris and its components, with emphasis on the characteristics of the blade.

Referring to the illustration (Figure 1) it will be seen that a typical kris consists of a blade, a sheath, a hilt and hilt-to-blade fittings. The blade, always of steel, may be straight or sinuous; the scabbard, usually of wood, may be encased fully or partially in metal or is sometimes fully or partially of ivory. The hilt, usually of wood or ivory, is sometimes found in silver or brass and, rarely, in gold or shell. The fittings are usually brass or copper, often silvered or gilded. Fittings of silver or gold are frequent, as are styles decorated with glass cabochons, or rough-cut gems.

Of course, the blade is the most important part of any sword. Granting the technical superiority of the Japanese blade over all others, and the excellence of good Persian blades, the kris blade yet shows greater artistry and imagination in the forging and decoration of its many complex forms. All three of these very different blades from quite different cultures are forged by procedures that are common in many respects.

The kris and early Persian blades were forged by a technique known as 'pattern welding'—one in which two or more layers of different steels were pounded together while red-hot, folded or twisted, pounded more and folded more until the desired number of layers, or laminae, were obtained. The rough sword blade so achieved was then filed and polished smooth and finally acid-etched to bring out the contrasting colours of the low and high-carbon steels. The decorative effect in good work is beautiful and fascinating and adds greatly to the value of the weapon (Figure 8).

The patterns so obtained may be controlled by a skilful smith who produces all sorts of fanciful designs. The designs range from misty and diaphanous to bold, three-dimensional textures. Some of their names are revealing: In krises we find 'rice grains' or 'nutmeg flowers'; in Persian work, a ladder pattern called 'forty steps'; in Japanese work a superb textured wood-grain effect called *mokume*, etc.

The term *pamor* is used to denote the Malay form of damascene markings. The word is Malay—originally meaning mixture or alloy. Now it is often used to describe the nickelous metal in the kris-marking process and just as often used to denote the variegated patterns produced by the *pamor* metal. To produce the effect, two or more dissimilar metals are used— an ordinary iron combined with a nickel-bearing iron of terrestrial, or preferably meteoric origin.

Early in kris history—*c.* 1600—it was found that if one of the metals contained nickel, the *pamor* showed sharply more contrast. Possibly at that time and certainly later nearly all nickelous iron came from the Celebes (Sulawesi) and was termed *pamor luwu*. Such iron was often called 'white iron' because being more etch-resistant it left silvery threads on an acid-darkened blade. Probably late in the eighteenth century the first kris blades were made containing nickelous iron from the meteor that had fallen near Prambanan in 1749. Groneman reports the nickel content of *pamor luwu* as 0.4 per cent and *pamor prambanan* as being 4.7 per cent. However, present day samples of the latter iron, on file in the Field Museum, Chicago, and in the British Museum, each assay a 9.4 percentage of nickel. The great difference in nickel content between the two irons *p.l.* and *p.p.*–results in far brighter and more contrasting designs in blades containing iron from the meteor. Furthermore, because the iron had arrived from the heavens, it was thought to impart magic and sanctity to a kris made from that holy substance. Natural iron deposits are virtually non-existent in Java, so that the very scarce meteor iron rose to exalted preference as the necessary ingredient in a really fine kris.

It seems too, in reviewing the history of the use of meteor iron in the kris, that we are seeing a legend in the process of creation. According to Bronson (1987), there is simply no evidence of krises being made from meteor iron prior to the nineteenth century. This suggests that the whole adoration of the meteor iron kris has caused its history to be distorted—that it is not a very old form of kris, and certainly not the original form. At the turn of the century–*c.* 1900–kris *empu* were using with good results European scrap iron in the form of bicycle parts and tools containing about 5 per cent nickel. In 1910 Groneman published a series of experiments using nickel sheets obtained from the Krupp mills in Germany. These laminae, sandwiched, folded and forged with ordinary iron, provided extremely bright *pamor* lines. However, sophisticated kris fanciers, did and still do prefer more subdued coloration in the *pamor* designs.

Blades containing pure nickel are termed *pamor nekel*. Blades containing terrestrial nickel are often described as *tajamnya tiga* (three-sharps)—that is sharp on each edge and at the point. A kris of meteor iron is called *tajamnya lima* (five-sharps) because the texture of *pamor* made with Prambanan meteor iron is sharp to the touch, thus providing two additional sharps.

We have compared the forging of kris blades to early Persian blades in a method called 'pattern-welding'. Rawson (1969) calls this 'mechanical damask' and relates that sometime in the seventeenth century a steel known as 'wootz', imported from

India, changed the method of forging Persian blades. A simple billet of wootz, when forged and cooled slowly, undergoes a transformation of its crystalline structure, which after being polished and etched produces a beautiful damask. This he terms 'crystalline damask' and comments on the superiority of blades so produced. Both types of damask are referred to as 'watered steel', a term used by collectors of arms and armour to denote any steel with damascene markings.

The finest example of controlled work in the forging of a sword blade is the Japanese blade. It too is fashioned by repeated foldings and hammerings of two different steels but usually the softer alloy is forged into a central core with the harder steel forming an envelope. The envelope or skin is then rough ground, tempered and finally finish-ground with a series of abrasive stones. The tempering process, done with a clay resist, ensures an extremely hard edge with a less hard, but tougher body. The line that joins the hard edge with the softer body of the blade is called the *yakiba* or temper line. It runs the full length of the blade and may take many predetermined aesthetic forms. The *yakiba* is often considered the finest example of damascening in a sword blade, but it should be noted that it is brought about by imposing uneven temperatures in the tempering process, rather than because of two dissimilar metals meeting at the temper line.

The kris blade is part of a family of blades that have the common feature of a *ganja*—otherwise the blades vary considerably. A Javanese blade is typically short and light-weight with rough-texture *pamor* due to ritual etching with lemon segments (Figure 6). A Balinese blade is typically longer, polished and acid-darkened to a gleaming blue-black with silvery whorls or threads running its length. A Sumatran blade is straight, usually long and thin, deadly looking. A Moro[1] kris is heavy

---

[1] Moros are the Muslim peoples of the Sulu and Mindanao islands in the Philippines.

33

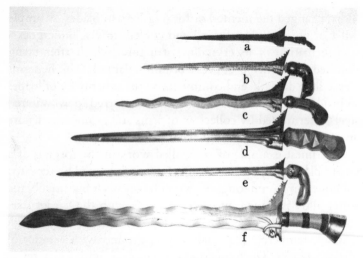

Figure 6. Kris Types and Comparative Blade Lengths. (a) Majapahit 9.8 inches; (b) Sumatra 12.7; (c) Java 14.8; (d) Bali 18.7; (e) Sumatra 19.9; (f) Mindanao Moro 22.5. Madura blade lengths approximate (b) length. These lengths may vary plus or minus ten per cent.

and long, broad, brightly polished, a combat weapon and jungle sword.

The blade is called *wilah* in Javanese, *mata* in Malay. It has three basic characteristics—*dapor*, *prabot* and *pamor* (Figure 7). *Dapor* denotes its general shape or outline. A straight blade is *dapor bener*; a sinuous blade is *dapor 'lok*—*'lok* being a Malay word for curve. The number of curves or waves in a kris blade are counted as *'lok*—five *'lok*, thirteen *'lok* etc. *'Lok* are counted by starting at the first concave curve near the base of the blade on its underneath side (Figure 1). The number of *'lok* are always odd, although in practice it is often difficult to distinguish the last small *'lok* at the tip of the blade.

Kris blades are generally classified by *dapor* characteristics but finer distinctions are made by considering details of the *prabot*.

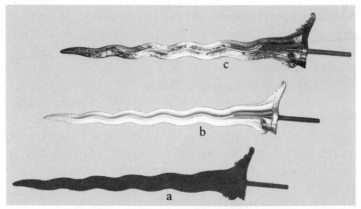

Figure 7. Blade Characteristics. (a) *dapor*: the outline and shape. (b) *prabot*: the chiselling and fine detail. (c) *pamor*: the damascene design.

The term *prabot* denotes the sculptured, chiselled or moulded features found at the base of the blade. In a well-made kris these features are considerable and intricate and because of their zoomorphic or mythological connotations add much interest to the study of the piece.

Some important elements of *prabot* detail are shown in the illustration of kris components (Figure 1): *belalai gajah*, elephant's trunk; *lambi gajah*, elephant's lips; *janggut*, serrations called 'beard'; *peksi*, the tang; *ganja*, the characteristic kris guard with *dagu* its short end, and *aring* its long end. The *sogokan* are the parallel grooves in a well-made blade, the *pecetan* is the hollow on the *dagu* side of these grooves. The *grening* are the dentiform frets on the *aring* end.

The number of forms of kris blades is surprising (Figures 5 and 6). Using only Javanese blades as an example because of the extensive literature that exists, one finds every gross and every subtle distinction identified and named. Raffles says the varieties exceed one hundred; he provides an illustrated plate of 41 'common' types. Groneman describes, in his masterful dissertations, 118 types, 40 of which are straight (*dapor bener*) and 78 sinuous (*dapor 'lok*). Holstein, working carefully to eliminate duplicates by reason of his unfamiliarity with the Javanese language, settled on 168 types, 64 of which have straight blades and 104 sinuous blades.

The subject of *pamor* in the kris would fill an entire volume, but a book of this size can only introduce the reader to its vast lore. *Pamor* forms a large part of the mystique of the kris. Its study, apart from the mechanical aspects of producing it, rewards the scholar with unexpected insight into bygone semi-primitive minds that saw particular earthly and unearthly wonders in the various designs.

The varieties of *pamor* are numerous. Groneman describes 48 styles, mostly in terse translated phrases suggestive of *haiku* poetry—'ripples in the water', 'roots in the air', etc. A current publication of the National Museum in Jakarta adds even more to the mystique of the blade with its descriptions of 70 styles of overall *pamor* and 52 individual small-design *pamor* markings. The individual *pamor* markings, called *pamor trap trappan*, are rare (Figure 8). Sometimes they appear accidentally in the over-all *pamor* but mostly they are hammered-on pieces of scarce *pamor* material. To each overall or individual *pamor* design is attributed some magic, mystic or allegorical quality. For example, one design, *pamor sumberan*, will 'give a profit'; another, *pamor mantri wasesa*, assures the owner he is 'safe everywhere'; still another, *pamor bulan bulan*, says, 'the enemy's eyes will blur'; and so forth.

Groneman concluded that nearly all *pamor* styles derive from five basic types. Other scholars appear to accept his findings with little question but his rationale would be better understood if he had offered more explanation on this specific subject.

Here are given the five basic *pamor* designs and the translation of their names:

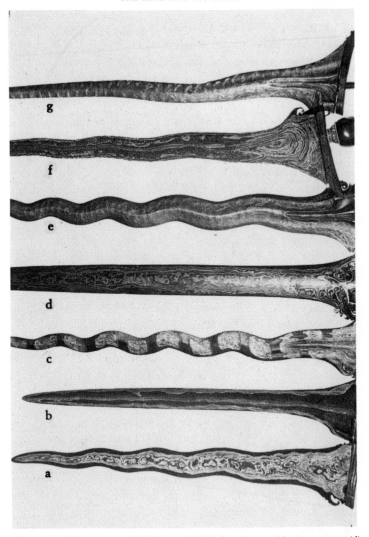

Figure 8. Various *Pamor*. (a) *beras wutah*; (b) *dwee warna*; (c) *trap-trappan*; (d) *kulit semangka*; (e) *udan mas*; (f) *pusaran ayer* (?); (g) *mayang mekar*. All blades Java except (d) Bali.

1.  *Pamor wos wutah*, scattered rice grains.
2.  *Pamor sekar pala*, nutmeg flowers.
3.  *Pamor sekar ngadeg*, straight standing flowers.
4.  *Pamor blarak ngirid*, parallel coconut leaves.
5.  *Pamor sekar temu*, ginger flowers.

The forging of the kris blade, an intricate and extensive process, is described in detail by others. Basically it consists of combining some form of *pamor—luwu*, *prambanan* or *nekel—* with lower irons and a harder steel cutting edge to create a multi-laminar sandwich which, when etched, reveals beautiful patterns. Some descriptions of this lengthy and often ritualistic process have led their authors to be criticized for writing excessively pedantic accounts of an otherwise interesting form of artistic skill. The blade-making process is indeed often a most complicated procedure and certainly that is so in a well-made Javanese blade. For that reason we will describe one of the simpler forms—the Balinese blade—which is nevertheless known for its particular style of beauty.

The smith prepares a thick rectangle or strap of iron which consists of three layers of thin *pamor* sandwiched with three layers of soft iron. While red-hot the strap is worked with a hammer so all layers are thoroughly fused together. In its working the strap becomes longer and thinner. The strap is folded to provide a long U-shape piece with the *pamor* side outside. The fold or bottom of the U is cut off; it will provide material for the *ganja*. A thin piece of steel or hard iron is inserted between the two legs of the U-shape strap. This hard core will provide a sharp point and hard edges to the kris. The tang is now worked up and out of the base of the whole. All is again heated and forged to a single rough blade.

The blade is now filed and shaped by hand. If the shape is *dapor 'lok*, the curves are hammered into the straight blade using heat and a cylindrical form. The numerous details of the *prabot* are added using small chisels and files. Next, the *ganja* is fashioned, using the cut-off piece from the base of the U-shape strap. Because it was part of the blade material, the *ganja* will have the same *pamor* design as the blade itself. Now the entire blade is polished on a whetstone and by hand using fine grit on a bamboo pad. After this the blade is treated with a mixture of arsenic and lemon juice. The acidic solution attacks and colours the iron a lustrous blue-black but leaves the nickelous threads and whorls unaffected. Finally, the blade is washed and protected against rust with an application of aromatic oil. Now the *pamor* appears as bright, silvery lines against the polished darker metal—an effect considered by many to be the most beautiful of all kris *pamor*.

The working of Javanese blades is far more complex. The *pamor* material is routinely laminated into thirty-two, sixty-four or more than a hundred layers, using two or three types of irons. The procedure consists of forging, severing, combining and reforging of the original billets of *pamor* and the irons to achieve fine and intricate configurations in the patterns. Further, this work is then transformed into three-dimensional or textured designs by repeated etchings, over long periods, with lemon segments and arsenic darkener. The rough, wood-grain effects, sometimes having a strange spongy appearance, seldom impresses the initiate. Eventually, with sufficient exposure to ordinary and superb blades one grows to admire the work and recognize Javanese style as the most skilled and controlled of all Malay *pamor*.

Blades similar to one another were forged in many places in the Malay Archipelago. Thus it is difficult to fix the origin of a kris by its blade alone. A few distinct types are readily identified—any fine Java blade, most Bali blades, all Sumatra executioners' blades and all Moro blades. Because of the constant trade and cultural exchange throughout the entire area—from Aceh in North Sumatra to Mindanao in the far Philippines—

one must examine a kris by all of its components. Good results will be obtained by studying the hilt form, sheath form, and hilt fittings, in that order of certainty. An accurate judgement of blade origin is more likely when following this procedure.

I (a) The Prambanan Meteor in the Kraton Garden at Surakarta.

(b) A close view.

## 2 Wedding Scenes

(a) (*right*) Menangkabau bridegroom with characteristic Sumatra kris. This is a superbly modelled figure. (Display: Chicago, Field Museum of Natural History)

(b) (*below*) Seated couple in a Sulawesi wedding ceremony. The figures are poorly modelled but the trappings are authentic and excellent. (Display: Paris, Musée de l' Homme)

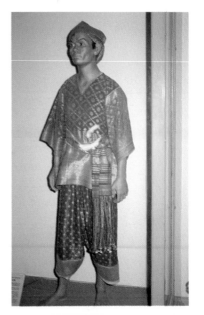

3 *Ramayana* Dancers

(a) (*above*) Arjuna and Domangjaja in an episode from the *Mahabharata*.

(b) (*left*) Srikandi is victorious in a kris duel with the Princess Suradewati. These re-enactments are performed throughout Java.

4 (a) (*above*) A Balinese painting depicting a Barong dance scene. Rangda, a malevolent demon (with long claws) mesmerizes her village attackers and causes them to turn their krises against themselves. Because they are under the protection of Barong (the huge animal demon), they are not wounded.

(b) (*right*) 'Yellow-Kris', a *wayang kulit* (shadow play) figure: Cirebon.

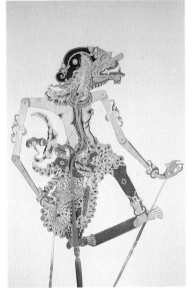

 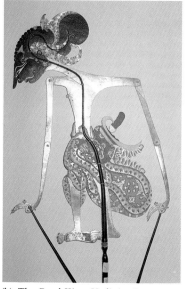

5 (a) Bancak, a Clown Figure:       (b) The Good King, Yudistira: Java.
Surakarta.

(c) A Great Battle Scene from the *Mahabharata*.

## 6 Gold Krises

(a) (*right*) Java kris, with Naga
blade and stemmed *mendak*. The
hilt is deeply incised Palembang
work.

(b) (*lower right*) Sulawesi kris with
Malacca cup *selut*. The gold loop is
called *toli-toli*.

(c) (*below*) Sulawesi kris with
Bugis *selut*.

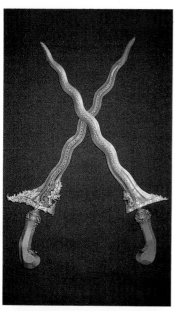

7 Gold Krises

(a) (*left*) Two Java krises, both with fine Naga blades, *mendak* and *selut*. The hilts are Surakarta style.

(b) (*lower left*) Two Peninsular krises, one with a Malacca cup *selut*, one with a Bugis cup.

(c) (*below*) The lower *pendok* and *buntut* of a fine Peninsular kris.

## 8 Kris Types

(a) *(right)* Java: sheath type *ladrang*; *wrangka* wood *kemuning*; *pendok* type *bunton*; hilt type Surakarta.

(b) *(lower right)* Java: sheath type *gayaman*; painted *wrangka* with *raksasa* (demon) face; *pendok* *blewah*; hilt type Yogyakarta.

(c) *(below)* Bali and Java: sheath types *sandang walikat*. The Java kris has an ivory Madura hilt.

## 9 Kris Types

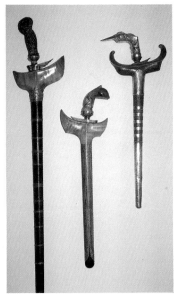

(a) (*left*) Two Bali krises, one with flaring *wrangka*, one with oblate *wrangka*. The ivory hilt is a grimacing *jawa sakit* figure; the gold figure is Bayu, his sheath is *kayu pelet*.

(b) (*lower left*) Two Madura krises. The carved dark wood *wrangka* are characteristic. One kris has a stemmed *mendak* with *pendok natang* (windowed).

(c) (*below*) Two Sumatra krises. The hilt and *wrangka* of the long kris are characteristic. The kris from Patani has a *hulu wayang* hilt.

(a) (*right*) Peninsular kris: *Jawa demam hulu*, Bugis cup *selut*. The sarong wood is *kemuning*.

(b) (*lower right*) Bugis (Sulawesi) kris. This example is characteristic in every feature except for the absence of the metal loop—the *toli-toli*.

(c) (*below*) Two Moro krises, Mindanao and Sulu. The cockatoo pommel is typical Sulu style. The Malay term *sundang* should not be used for Moro krises, as in the Philippines the word denotes an agricultural tool. Borneo Malays use the term *sulok*.

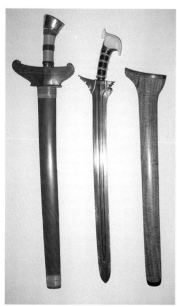

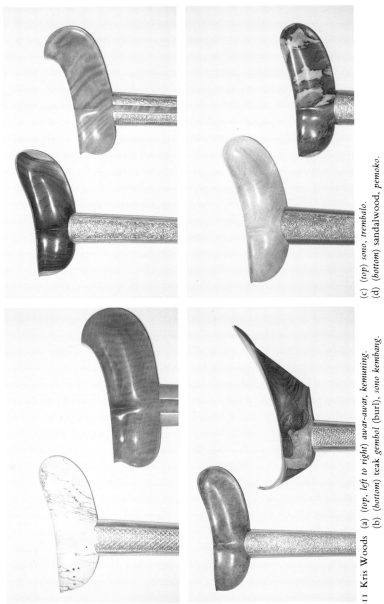

11 Kris Woods (a) (top, left to right) awar-awar, kemuning.
(b) (bottom) teak gembol (burl), sono kembang.
(c) (top) sono, trembalo.
(d) (bottom) sandalwood, pemoko.

12  Hilt Fittings  (a) (top, left to right) Bali selut and mendak.
          (b) (bottom) Bugis cups, one in gold.

(c) (top) Java mendak and selut, Madura mendak.
(d) (bottom) Two Malacca cups, a stemmed mendak.

## 13 Kris Art

(a) (*right*) A description of blade shapes (*dapor*) in old Javanese script, from the museum library at Yogyakarta.

(b) (*lower right*) A resting place for a family heirloom: Menangkabau. The kris is a Peninsular type with Sumatran decoration.

(c) (*below*) Naga (serpent) blades: Java, Madura, Bali. The Madura kris (*centre*) is a recent forgery. The Naga profiles, made from an old spear-head, have been welded on. Grooves have been cut in the blade to simulate the snake's body.

(a) (*right*) A Balinese prince.

(b) (*lower right*) A Chinese Buddhist mendicant. Chinese figures are frequently found. The cord-wrapped hilt is common, the scabbard type is *sandang walikat*: Bali.

(c) (*below*) Frog figure: Bali. The *wrangka* is the flap (flat) type, the *gandar* is *kayu pelet*.

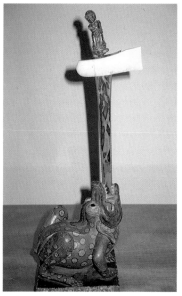

## 15 Kris Holders

(a) (*left*) The figure is Bima, a Hindu demi-god: Bali.

(b) (*lower left*) A rare Javanese kris board. Cord loops hold two krises. The figures are *wayang* characters. Poly-chromed wood.

(c) (*below*) A Bali *legong* dancer. The patterned wood zigzag hilt is common.

(d) (*far below*) The demon Nawa Sari holding a sheaf of rice behind his head. The small kris hilt is similarly carved.

(a) (*left*) A concrete effigy of an
old *kraton* guard in a hotel garden
in Yogyakarta.

(b) (*below*) An attendant
scheduling dance and *wayang*
programmes at the old *kraton*
grounds in Yogyakarta. He is
wearing the kris in the Javanese
manner.

# 6

# The Sheath, Hilt and Fittings

THE Javanese say that a kris should be drawn from its sheath carefully and with respect. It should be replaced in the same manner and thus kept from harm or abuse. There is mysticism in the sheath as well as in the blade. Rassers (1940) suggests that the broad upper portion of a kris sheath is symbolic of a 'moon boat', the abode of Panji, the Javanese culture hero. Perhaps so, but there are also some practical considerations for that strange shape.

The sheath of a kris is usually light in weight and not very sturdy. The wood itself is often selected for its ornamental appeal rather than for its strength. However, kris sheaths cannot be considered flimsy as they all seem to be fitted together well. In addition, they are carried in a wide band or sash close to the body, which manner surely offers adequate protection to the sheath and its contents. The upper portion or mouth of the sheath is made large to receive the flaring *ganja* and to ensure that the sheath will remain in position when thrust into the sash or waistband (Plate 16b).

There are many styles of sheath, which when recognized become an important means of identifying krises. In the illustrations will be seen three types of Javanese sheath, four types of Balinese, three Sumatran, two Moro and one each Peninsular Malaysian and Madurese types (Plates 8–10). Of course, there are offshoots and variations, but most kris sheaths fall within these stylistic forms.

The sheath is called *sarong* in Malay, *wrangka* in Javanese. Because of the variety of dialects spoken throughout the archipelago, the components of a kris may be referred to by many names. There is also often no consistency in these names, for different authors do not always use the same terms for kris components from the same region. Therefore the terms used here are selected for the broadest reference value when compared to other literature. They are terms most frequently found—the use of which seems logical although drawn from more than a single language.

The *sarong* or complete sheath is composed of a wide upper part called the *wrangka*, and a lower shank called the *gandar*. The *wrangka* is always carved of a single piece of wood or ivory, sometimes horn, hollowed-out to receive its portion of the kris anatomy. The *gandar* is also made from a single hollowed-out piece; its top is tenoned to fit into the opening on the underside of the *wrangka*. Glue secures it. Long Sumatran *gandar* usually consist of two pieces glued or bound together with decorative metal bands. Often the joint is not at the edge of the sheath as expected but down its centre-line, front and back. For Sulu Moro and Philippine Moro krises the entire sheath, comprising *wrangka* and *gandar*, consists of two flat pieces glued or bound together with rattan. When the entire sheath of a kris is made from a single piece of hollowed-out material it is recognized as something special and is termed *sarong iras* or *wrangka iras*. Such sheaths are quite rare—particularly so if made of ornamental wood, as large pieces of patterned woods were difficult to find.

Most Javanese krises are fitted with a metal sleeve over the *gandar*. The sleeve is called the *pendok*; its tip is called the *buntut*. The *pendok* is found in three styles—*bunton* (closed), *blewah* (slotted) and *natang* (windowed). The *natang* style may have a decorative metal or tortoise shell insert showing through the window. The insert is called a *slorok* (Figure 9). Sometimes a sheath from Bali or Madura will display a demon face, usually Bonaspati, at the top of its *pendok*, in which case the *pendok* is called *topengen* (*topeng*, 'mask').

Ornamental woods of many varieties were used for kris sheaths (Plate 11). The woods were scarce and the searchers for

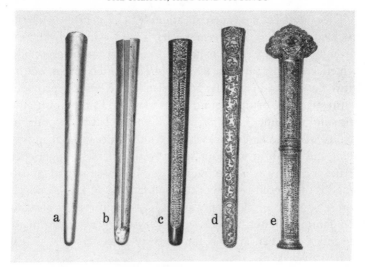

Figure 9. Types of *Pendok*. (a) *bunton*; (b) *blewah*; (c) *natang* with removable *slorok*; (d) *natang* pierced through; (e) *topengen*; (a), (b), (c), Java; (d) Bali; (e) Bali demon motif with Bugis *buntut*.

such woods belonged to a special profession in Bali and southeast Java. Sometimes hundreds of trees were notched to find one bearing a patterned patch of sufficient size to make a whole sheath, a *sarong iras*. Sheath and hilt crafting was an art, each with its own masters. The materials were often rare and valuable and krises so fitted brought higher prices.

A fine Balinese sheath often includes a *wrangka* (upper part) showing wood-grain of some distinction matched to a similarly grained veneer-plate cemented to the front of the *gandar* (Plates 9a, and 14a, c). The wood is often *sono*, a dark variety resembling walnut with a curvy grain; if more burl-like it is called *sono kembang* (flowered wood). Often the *wrangka* is painted or gilded—in which case the *gandar* veneer-plate and hilt may be of nicely marked light-hued wood known as *kayu pelet* (speckled wood).

The *wrangka* of a Javanese sheath may be of *awar awar*, a light speckled variety of the *timaha* species. Two woods well-known throughout the area, *kemuning* and *trembalo*, provide especially rich effects on the Javanese *wrangka* or, as is often found, on the entire sheath of a Peninsular Malaysian kris. *Kemuning* provides a lustrous flame or tiger-grain effect identical to the finish on a fine smoking-pipe (Plates 8a, 11a). *Trembalo* has the wondrous quality of chatoyancy[1] which makes the discovery of movement and depth in its grain an especially pleasing experience (Plate 11c). However, the fragrant and honey-coloured sandalwood is the favourite of workers and fanciers of kris woods. It is in reasonably ample supply and it is easy to carve. Its pleasant and familiar odour is welcome everywhere as an aromatic reminder of Asian art and the faraway places from which it comes (Plate 11d).

\* \* \*

The probable origins of the kris are better traced through study of its hilt than by any other characteristic. The hilt is termed *hulu* in Malay, *ukiran* in Javanese. It takes many mythological, anthropomorphic and zoomorphic forms that offer valuable evidence (or at least, clues) to the culture that produced the kris. Probably the culture was Javanese under strong Hindu influence, since those idol-like hilt figures that can be identified are usually from the Hindu pantheon of gods. Ravana and Ganesa are often depicted, Vishnu and Shiva less frequently. Garuda, the mount and carrier of Vishnu, is most common; it is found in myriad versions, about which reams of conjecture have been written.

The earliest kris which shows an anthropomorphic figure is, of course, the Majapahit kris. There exist many examples of this small dagger, all showing an iron hilt continuous with the blade

[1] A changeable, undulating lustre, like that of a cat's eye in the dark.

44

The Balinese hilt offers the most variety for study of origins. In the fifteenth century, the last Hindu-Javanese empire, Majapahit, fell to the ever-increasing strength of the Muslim world. By Islamic law the depiction of living images was prohibited in art or utilitarian articles. This constraint was felt throughout all centres of artistic endeavour and, over the ensuing years caused a considerable exodus of artists, artisans and dissidents in general, to remaining Hindu areas such as Bali, Madura and Lombok. It is in those areas, Bali particularly, that one finds images in purer form—figures that have not been modified or abstracted to circumvent Islamic proscriptions against imagery in art.

A good working knowledge of hilt types throughout Malaysia and Indonesia will serve the collector well. In addition, it will provide another avenue to the better understanding of all art from those areas. The principal forms of Bali hilts will be seen in the illustrations (Figure 10, Plates 14 and 15). The most ornamental of the Bali types is a large upright figure made of a carved wood or mastic effigy covered with gold foil or gold-plated copper foil (Plates 9a, 14a and c). Sometimes this type of hilt is of cast brass which has been polished and engraved. The mythological figure may take many forms. Most often found is Bayu, who carries, in an ornate vase held waist high, a holy fluid, *amrita* (sanskrit, 'immortal') which brings good fortune and is exhalted symbolically by a gem set into the vase. Usually also, there is a profusion of semi-precious stones or glass cabochons set into these gold figures. Sometimes the demi-god, Nawa Sari is seen; he has one arm raised to the back of his head, usually but not always, grasping a sheaf of rice (Plate 15d). Ravana, enemy of Rama, abductor of his wife, the lovely Sita, may be found. He has a large head, a particularly ferocious countenance with long tusks and may be brandishing a sword or dagger.

Bali hilts tend to be large, as the Bali kris itself is often large and heavy. Massive wooden hilts are common; a noteworthy type is a zigzag cubist or 'pleated' style that never ceases to cause speculation as to the intent of its design (Plate 15c). Often this hilt is made of a pale decorative wood such as *kayu pelet* selected to provide a single dark band across its centre. Another wood, *sono kembang*, showing rich-toned dark and light colours is always pleasing. Both woods are particularly attractive when found *en suite* with the wood of the sheath.

Krises from the island of Madura are frequently fitted with ivory hilts carved in intricate floral patterns (Figure 10, Plate 12c). The mode, called *gaya kembang* (flower style) is unique in that these hilts are further adaptations of the severely stylized Javanese hilt. This seems to be a reversal of the typical stylizing sequence, because here a new style has emerged which is equivalent in originality and detail to the old form. The handsome Madura hilts most often show overall floral carving—tendrils, leaves and blossoms filling every space. Others are done with an eye to geometry and show orderly design elements of chevrons, spaced leafy sprays, knobby grids, and sometimes, a Chinese key border. Occasionally a strangely abstracted face, barely discernible, can be made out in the details of the carving (Figure 10).

It is difficult to separate some Madura figural hilts from similar Java hilts. Generally, ivory Madura hilts are bent over more; the themes are usually abstracted demi-god figures, sometimes animals, rather than subjects from mythology. The Madura ivory carving is better executed. European motifs are often found. The hilt may be capped with a Greek helmet, it may display a panoply of pole-arms, epaulets may be discerned at its 'shoulders'. A crown or winged horse displayed frontally is frequent. They are said to be symbols of the royal house but one should not so assume if the carving is of ordinary or inferior quality.

Javanese kris hilts take many forms, some of which are

consistently misjudged by keeper and collector alike. From north-west Java and south-east Sumatra come older, more ornate adaptations of figures from Hindu mythology (Figure 10). From Central Java comes the elegant and highly refined *kraton* style (Figure 11). From East Java comes the odd-looking ivory or bone drill-carved conical shrubs referred to as 'corn' style (Figure 10). Because the island of Madura lies just one and a half miles off the north-east coast of Java, the identification of North Java hilts is complicated by the influence of Madura styles.

There are four categories of Javanese hilts into which most specimens will fit (Figures 10 and 11).

*Northern Floral* Resembling the Madura style but with important differences. The hilt is nearly upright, rarely curled over; the carving is less floral and more geometric; it is sometimes carved with the point of a rotating drill. It is usually of ivory, sometimes of wood.

*Eastern Floral* Resembling a conical shrub or corn ear or any similar amorphous shape. Often, but not always drill-carved. Most examples are of ivory or bone.

*Cirebon (and Lampong) Figural* Taking the form of a mytho-logical figure—Garuda, Ganesa and a *wayang* face being common. The figures are most often bent over in a brooding position and are often stylized to near extinction. They are usually of dark, hard wood; sometimes of ivory.

*Kraton Style* From Surakarta, Yogyakarta and East Java. A hilt of plain rubbed wood having seven planar sides. All evidence of animate form is abstracted away leaving only a small *kala* mask. The Surakarta style is longer and bent over with a tiny 'nose' (*kuncung*, pronounced 'kunchung') protrud-ing from the *kala* face. The Yogyakarta style is shorter, more erect and does not show the *kuncung*. Eastern style is a short, swollen type with *kuncung*. It often displays a decorative band in its wood grain and is sometimes mistaken for a similar Bali hilt.

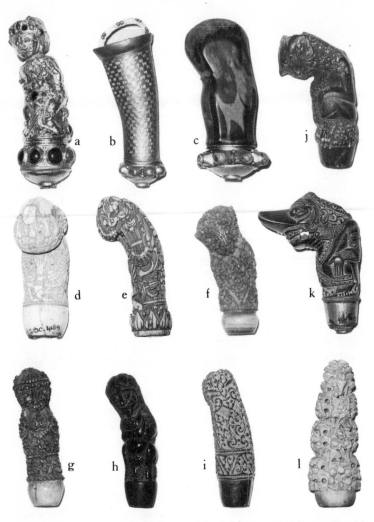

Figure 10. Types of Hilts (a) Bali gold figure, Bayu; (b) Bali metallic; (c) Bali wood, Java style (compare with 11c); (d) Madura ivory floral with Royal horse; (e) Madura floral; (f) Madura figural; (g) Madura, sometimes north coast Java; (h) north coast Java, sometimes Madura; (i) Java, northern floral; (j) Sumatra, Lampong Garuda figure; (k) Cirebon, wayang figure; (l) Java, eastern floral, corn style.

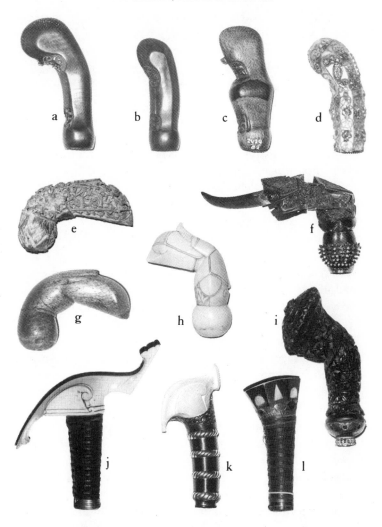

Figure 11. Types of Hilts. (a) Java, *kraton* style; Surakarta; (b) Yogyakarta; (c) Surakarta eastern; (d) East Java metallic with gems; (e) Sumatra; (f) Patani, *wayang* figure; (g) Sulawesi; (h) Peninsular Malaysia *jawa demam* figure (compare angle of inclination of (h) (e) (g)); (i) Sumatra erect floral type; (j) Sulu Moro Regent style; (k) Sulu cockatoo type; (l) Mindanao Moro.

Nowadays, the wood used for most hilts is *kemuning*, a lustrous grained wood of medium colour. It is stained a deep red prior to polishing. Sometimes an exotic dark wood *tayuman* is found and formerly, fine krises were fitted with hilts of *kayu cukila*, a wood found growing on the slopes of the volcano Sumbing.

The Surakarta style of kris hilt is surely the most beautiful single element in all of Indonesian art. It has an elegance, a grace and simplicity that defies description of sufficient subtlety to do justice to its exquisite form. No picture captures its spirit; its seven smooth planes are lost to tactile sense. The beauty of its austere form and delicate carvings is not well shown in flat illustrations. Only a keeper or collector of these pieces can know them well, and, as in the case of Javanese *pamor*, familiarity causes one to succumb to the charm of the elegant *ukiran*.

Because of its flat sides the hilt is referred to as 'planar'. Except for the *patra*, the carvings on the inside faces, the hilt is otherwise unadorned. The *patra* are similar to the *kala* (demon) masks known as *tao-tieh* on Chinese bronzes and are curiously like the Arctic Haida and Tlingit totem figures. No doubt some long-distant Chinese mythology binds together these widely separated mystic faces. Groneman sees the *wayang* face in these masks; this author doubts a connection between the two images.

Much has been written about the *hulu*, the hilt of the Peninsular Malaysian kris. It is usually in the form of a highly abstracted crouching or squatting figure which is holding its sides as if in distress (Figure 11h). The position is known as *jawa demam* (fever stricken), *jawa gigil* (shivering) or *jawa sakit*. Considerable speculation concerns its origin—whether it is indeed an aspect of the Hindu bird-god Garuda, carrier of Vishnu; a zoomorphic evolution of some god-figure stemming from the Majapahit hilt or simply a variation of the cockatoo, the parrot, a common design element positively identified on many Malayan hilts.

In its earliest and purest form, as found in Lampong, South

Sumatra, it is a seated figure with bulging eyes and bird beak, hands on knees and curly hair falling to its waist (Figure 10j). Sometimes the figure shows a Naga, a serpent, hung about its neck, corroborating the legend that Garuda was enemy of the Nagas and, in a great battle, destroyed all but one which he displays as evidence of his powers.

However most *hulu* are so abstracted that the figure can easily be regarded as a stylized cockatoo. This rationale is strengthened by many good examples of *hulu kakatua* in Malaysian krises and in Sulu Moro krises. In the Sulu style of hilt almost every example can be regarded as an adapted head of the cockatoo. There is greater variety in Philippine Moro hilts (Figure 11).

A form of hilt of unusual artistry and cultural associations is a spectacular style from Patani (to the north of Peninsular Malaysia). Because of its exaggerated long nose, it is popularly nicknamed *hulu pekaka*–kingfisher hilt. However its bulging eyes, grinning teeth and distinct resemblance to classic figures in Javanese drama justify the more appropriate term *wayang* style (Figure 11). The hilt is noteworthy for its conformity to old values in design detail and mythological connection, yet it is rendered in a style that is surprising and delightful to all who view it.

\*     \*     \*

The decorative metal rings that come between the base of the hilt and the blade of a kris are often in themselves little works of art. They vary widely from island to island yet similarities exist across vast distances that cause puzzlement to the scholar. Balinese and Javanese fittings cause few problems as they are distinctive to their regions. Fittings from other areas are not always so easily identified, but the problem is simplified if one remembers two basic facts of cultural distribution within the Malay Archipelago.

One was the movement of Bugis seamen and traders from the Celebes (Sulawesi) west and north to Sumatra and Singapore, through the Straits of Malacca and on to Penang. Another influence was the continuing intercourse between Peninsular Malaysia and the island of Sumatra. As far as the kris is concerned these trade patterns have left their mark. Peninsular krises are generally of Sulawesi form but sometimes reflect Sumatran styles. Some Sumatran krises baffle the collector because of their similarity to Sulawesi types. Madura and North Coast Java krises are often confused and it is hopeless to search for a typical Borneo kris. A Borneo kris may be any of the styles brought to its endless coastline by all of the cultures surrounding it.

The Malayan term for a hilt fitting is *pendongkok*. The Javanese term is *mendak* for a small transition piece and *selut* for a larger fitting which forms a cup around the base of the hilt. *Mendak* and *selut*, because they refer to a fitting that is smaller than the hilt or to one that is larger, are good terms for all fittings whatever their origin. Hilt fittings may be classified into six basic groups:

*Bali style* A circular band set with cabochon gemstones. It is found in two diameters—the small size just fits over the tang of the blade, the larger size may exceed the diameter of the hilt at its base (Plate 12a).

*Java style* Two forms are common, the *mendak* and the *selut*. The *mendak* is found on most Java krises. It is a small conical cup usually made of gilded copper. There are three styles of this cup. It may be a plain polished casting of brass; a built-up assembly of tiny metal rings, prongs and balls; or a similarly constructed assembly ornamented with delicate filigree gold-work or set with poorly faceted gemstones (Plate 12c). A *mendak* from Madura is usually a simply-formed conical shell decorated with filigree work. It is not an assembly of separate rings as is the Java *mendak* (Plate 12c).

The *selut* is the larger of the two Java fittings. It is a true aesthetic continuation of the *ukiran*, the Javanese hilt. A properly carved *ukiran* swells at its base to blend its curve with the contours of the *selut*. The tapering *mendak* completes the transition to the blade to provide a most handsome appearance. The *selut* is a hollow shell sometimes nicely engraved. Often it is of silver pierced through in a floral motif and set with gemstones. A matching ensemble of *selut* and *mendak* always denotes a fine kris (Plates 8a, 12c).

*Bugis (or Sulawesi) style* A flat cup with a thick wall, usually with a short stem and engraved in a floral or leafy motif. It is most often found in brass on ordinary krises; in finely detailed gold on special krises. Most krises from Sulawesi and Peninsular Malaysia bear this fitting; occasionally it is found on Sumatra krises (Plate 12b).

*Malacca cup style* A deep cup with a thin wall usually crafted to resemble a budding flower or leafy cup. Often it is of gold or silver pierced in fine detail; it may have a long stem or short base. This type of fitting is found on many Sumatra krises, particularly the long and slender *keris panjang*. Best examples are found on Peninsular krises of high quality especially if mounted with a *hulu wayang* (so called 'kingfisher' hilt). This fitting is often found on Sulawesi krises (Plate 12d).

Two Sumatran fittings (Figure 12) are sometimes found. The Sumatra cup is a tapering cylindrical socket which receives the base of the hilt. It is usually of nicely worked metal, often with a small pedestal base. Sometimes this fitting is found on older north coast Java krises thus linking Cirebon and Lampong hilt styles. Another fitting, the Sumatra *selut*, is more rare but easily recognized. It is a one-piece shell which tapers from hilt diameter to stem diameter in a graceful ogee curve. It is usually of engraved metal and always of Sumatran origin.

Finally, there exists a hilt fitting which may be termed a stemmed *mendak*. It is a small fitting without the complexity

a   b

Figure 12. Sumatran Fittings. (a) Sumatra cup with pedestal base; (b) Sumatra *selut*.

of a Javanese *mendak*. It is found in plain or decorated metal or ivory, usually with an attached stem (Plate 12d). Most often it is seen on smaller krises from Sumatra and Malaysia, sometimes from Java and Madura.

The art of the kris includes various accessories designed for its proper care. In Sumatra and Malaysia a *keris pusaka* (heirloom kris) merited a special cushion for its repose (Plate 13b). In Java, krises of particular worth were often displayed on a wooden wall plaque carved in a viny or floral way or carved and painted with a *wayang* theme (Plate 15b). Krises of important families were sometimes stored in a fine cabinet built for that purpose. The best of this type of art comes from Bali. There the superb Balinese woodcarvers produced a unique sculptured figure for holding one or two krises. The figures are found in human or god-figure form, often benign in aspect but sometimes with a monstrous or ogre-like face (Plate 15d). Some of the carvings are most imaginative in their depiction of unlikely creatures grasping, or in some way, holding a kris (Plate 14c). These colourful accoutrements add much to the understanding of the art of the kris and to the special care given to it by Malays everywhere.

# 7
# Preserving the Kris

FROM the preceding chapters the thoughtful reader will see that the kris is less a weapon than an important art object distinctive to Malay and Indonesian cultures. This idea is certainly reflected in the ever-rising prices of good krises in the art and auction markets. The value of these pieces is further increased by a general awakening, on a global scale, to the particular beauty of Malay and Indonesian art.

Today, the cult of the kris is kept alive principally on the island of Java, where it is perpetuated by many collectors' clubs and followers of the art. These groups meet regularly to compare and discuss their krises, particularly new acquisitions. They vie with each other in their search for fine old blades and in their careful restoration by traditional methods. These enthusiastic collectors take great pride in displaying their old blades set in lavish fittings made to specification by a few remaining craftsmen. At such meetings one often sees breathtaking ensembles of filigree gold and diamonds, mythological images painted in exquisite shades of lacquer, and woods and ivories of every rare form. More so than the museum of the world, it is the kris fanciers of Java that are keeping alive this specialized art.

The crafting of fine kris blades has virtually ceased. Most of the old smiths, the *empu*, have died; few are followed by trained assistants capable of carrying on their masters' fine work. However, a good kris, made to technical and magical specifications, can still be ordered in Central Java, and not at great expense considering the special skill of the *empu* developed during a lifetime of meticulous forging of red-hot irons. Besides the forging, he puts into the blade any combination of magical properties that can be agreed upon. Currently such a kris can be purchased for less than one week's salary of the average Western visitor.

In 1985, the Department of Art of New York University hosted a meeting of experts of sword steels. The meeting was called principally to report on and explore the renewed interest, worldwide, in wootz steel–both as an ancient Indian art form and for its modern-day use as fine steel in cutlery (see p. 32). The symposium was well attended by skilled metalworkers and related experts from Europe, India, and the United States. Among the exhibits displayed by these masters of the forged blade were replica swords and modern cutlery of wootz steel, replica Japanese blades of both *katana* (long sword) and *aikuchi* (dagger) styles, and indeed a magnificent replica, reconstructed from radiographs, of the great sword found in 1939 at the Sutton Hoo burial site in Suffolk, England.

Yet, for all the fine examples of technical perfection displayed at this meeting, none included the particular artistry that makes a kris the mystic weapon that it is. In the author's judgement, the kris is a better example of artistry in metalwork than in any other weapon. It is true artistry as opposed to superb technical skill alone which is often found in the working of metals by different peoples. The *empu* puts into the kris far more than just dexterity and judgement of physical properties. His belief in the mystic significance of what he is doing sets him apart from other smiths. His swords are magic swords, and in his often exalted state at his incandescent forge he forges his beliefs into that hot blade. For a special kris he prepares himself physically and emotionally through ritual procedures handed down from smith to smith. Only on prescribed days can he create his best work and often only at specific times of the day. His selection of the iron constituents of the blade is meticulous; some ingredients have more magical properties than others.

When these are combined into a specific blade shape with a pre-determined *pamor* pattern, any mystic property can be achieved. During the process, offerings of fruit and flowers are made to facilitate the transmutation of metal to magic.

All of these considerations define the subjective process in the making of a kris. As can be seen, much of the process includes personal idiosyncrasy based on the supernatural, thus taking kris-making out of the context of metalworking as it is usually understood. One dictionary definition of fine art is, 'that in which mind and imagination are chiefly concerned'. Thus, although it may seem excessive to bestow the term artist on a mere skilled metalworker, the subjective aspects of kris-making merit that term.

\*　　\*　　\*

The scant knowledge shown by collectors in respect to proper care of their valuable pieces is surprising. Yet, an observant acquisitor soon notices that items in his or her collection, kept in a seemingly static environment, undergo both subtle and gross changes. Pieces warp, joints come loose, or mildew gathers. Worse, colours fade, severe cracks develop, or heavy moulds form. In some cases, insects or their larvae find a comfortable home in the recesses of a valuable old piece and eventually do much internal damage. With minimal knowledge and attention, all of these distressing changes can be prevented. Therefore, it seems fitting to include in these writings some conservation procedures pertaining to collections of krises and related articles. Much of this advice applies to any collection containing items of organic (natural) substances, and some of the information applies to metallic artefacts of any type.

Museums are generally more familiar with conservation techniques since they are customarily entrusted with the preservation of fragile or perishable artefacts. A museum may have a wide assortment of organic and inorganic materials in its collections which require some knowledge of the effects of humidity, temperature, actinic rays, chemical irritants, pH factor, and vibrations on its fragile pieces. More and more we read of instances of deterioration of valuable art discovered by startled keepers. Those newsworthy instances usually involve famous or valuable old pieces and are really 'tip of the iceberg' examples of conditions as they actually exist in many collections.

Humidity, in various aspects–too high, too low, or fluctuating–is the factor most responsible for changes in articles on display or in storage. Organic substances are hygroscopic, that is, they absorb moisture freely. When an article of ivory, horn, or wood absorbs too much moisture it will swell and may crack; if the humidity is too low it may dry out the article causing it to shrink, warp, or crack. In addition, high humidity promotes the formation of mildew and of foxing (reddish-brown stains) of the surfaces affected. High humidity to the point of moist environment promotes heavy growth of destructive moulds and encourages the proliferation of vermin.

Despite the problems that high humidity may cause, far more damage occurs because of fluctuating moisture levels in the air. Organic materials not only absorb moisture freely, but they also release that moisture. In a sense such materials are continuously breathing. The breathing is slow; as moisture in the air increases, the object slowly absorbs it, swelling in the process. When moisture in the air decreases, the artefact gives up some of its moisture and shrinks in size. Because hygroscopic action converts to powerful physical movement, the principal is used in the manufacture of humidity controlling devices. It is this same powerful movement, on a miniscule scale, that is taking place in the cells and interstices of organic materials stored in an uncontrolled atmosphere. Ivory, horn, wood, leather, plant fibre, cloth, and paper are the usual materials subject to this breathing process. Because of the rigidity of their cell structures, ivory, horn, and wood develop cracks. The reaction may be different with more flexible materials. Painted surfaces often craze or pigment comes loose. In cloth objects, 'tone' or body is lost; with paper, buckling occurs.

Ideally, objects in a collection should be kept in a room or cabinet in which the humidity is controlled to some judicious level. Fifty-five per cent relative humidity is a practical level; 45 per cent is perhaps ideal but difficult to maintain continuously. According to some conservationists, 60 per cent relative humidity is safe if not allowed to fluctuate. For the private collector or small commercial gallery, some simple procedures are recommended. Assuming the collection is kept in a closed cabinet or a closed room, equip the enclosure with a thermometer and a humidity indicator. Maintain the temperature at a comfortable level—70–76 °F. Try to maintain the relative humidity at 45–55 per cent. In winter time, place a dish or bowl of water in the cabinet to raise the humidity level (museums frequently do this). Place larger tubs of water and some live plants in the display room. Since these procedures require frequent monitoring, it is often best to purchase a small commercially available humidifier which will eject a fine spray of water into the room's atmosphere and automatically respond to the degree of moisture required. During the summer season or in moist, hot climates, the reverse procedure is required. Maintain temperature as advised above. This is particularly important as cool air holds less moisture than hot air. Purchase, in this case, a small portable de-humidifier—these are commercially available everywhere—which will control relative humidity to any desired level.

The advice given here in respect to excess moisture applies also to ferrous objects such as kris and other sword blades. Many collectors, upon opening a drawer long undisturbed, have viewed with dismay the accumulation of rust on a beautifully damascened sword blade. Usually such corrosion causes permanent harm to the metal surface with the result that the surface cannot easily be restored to its original beauty. In the case of a fine Japanese sword, special abrasive stones and great skill are required to restore a blade damaged by corrosion. However, restoration is easier for most kris blades because of their textured *pamor* rather than polished surface.

Temperature swings are also responsible for damage to articles in a collection. In this respect, artefacts are subject to powerful expansion and contraction forces by reason of extreme temperatures alone, no moisture factors being involved. Such extremes often cause looseness at the joints of dissimilar materials of an assembly, and flaking of pigments, the cause, in this case, being the different rates of thermal expansion of unlike materials. Here, heat, or lack of it, converts to powerful movement. The principal is put to use in the manufacture of temperature controlling devices. High temperatures alone are damaging. They may bake out resins and other adhesives, cause colours to fade, embrittle paper and cellulose fibres, and otherwise hasten the normal oxidation process of all organic materials when in contact with the atmosphere. For these reasons, temperatures must be controlled to avoid extremes at the storage place. Collections should not be stored in unheated garages or cold outbuildings. In tropical ambients, a collection must be similarly protected against the effects of prolonged extreme heat.

Bright light is another factor in the deterioration of articles in a collection. All picture galleries are aware of this potential spoiler of fine art and take precautions to protect paintings from bright sunlight, and in the case of old and very valuable pieces, all bright light. The culprits here are actinic rays—short wave rays of the ultra-violet region which have a photo-chemical effect on pigments. These harmful rays may weaken or fade colours in new work, or cause deterioration in the colours in old work. Ordinary window glass filters out much ultra-violet light; nevertheless, pieces in a collection should never be displayed where sunlight may fall upon them. Prolonged exposure to sunlight will result in faded pigments and bleached surfaces, and nothing can be done to correct such damage. Krises are particularly likely to suffer damage from actinic rays because of the subtle coloration of the fine woods used for their scabbards and hilts (see p. 11). A fine lacquered kris, rare in any collection, will suffer even more when exposed to harsh sunlight.

In summing up the causes for deterioration of organic substances, it can be seen that moisture, temperature, and sunlight, when unregulated, are the reasons. These factors are generally well known by museum keepers and it will serve the individual well to heed and apply this knowledge to his own province of collecting. If the collector has no spirit for the bother and detail attendant to good conservation measures he or she should, at the very least, heed old and common advice which applies particularly in this case: 'keep in a cool, dry place, out of direct sunlight'.

\*     \*     \*

The preceding paragraphs describe a safe environment for a collection of krises or of articles of similar materials. These precautions ensure that items in storage or on display will not further deteriorate or, at least, that their rate of deterioration will be reduced to a negligible level. Now it seems appropriate to consider the best ways to prepare articles for display—ways to clean and renovate pieces selected for special attention.

Every acquisitor has, more than once in his collecting career, shaken his head in disbelief at someone's inept attempt to repair a fine piece. Most commonly, a wrong glue is used resulting in an unsightly repair or reseparation of the repaired joint. Frequently, over-zealous polishing removes surface gold and silver from repousse brass or delicately crafted copper fittings. With weapons, fire-gilding[1] and *koftgari*[2] work are particularly vulnerable as the gold (or silver) used in these techniques is often applied in thin leaf form. The edges of softer materials—wood, horn, etc.—are often buffed excessively thus destroying the crisp style intended by the craftsman. Most Javanese *ukiran* have been altered in this way.

Many sword collectors like to restore their old blades but proceed without skill and with damaging results. Their idea often is to achieve the shiniest surface possible, a chrome-plated look, an effect entirely inconsistent with Asian weapons art. These enthusiasts may wire-wheel kris blades or use abrasive papers on the contours of Japanese blades, thus effectively removing the precise textures, edges, and finishes fashioned by the skilled metalsmith. Often unsuitable oils or greases are applied to delicate steel surfaces. Oils intended to loosen rusted bolts or greases designed to protect military equipment contain additives that may corrode or discolour finely finished steels.

Little is known to the Western world about care of the kris blade. *Pamor* is strange stuff to the eye trained to see the absolute perfection of a Japanese blade or the fine watered steels (see p. 33) of Middle Eastern arms. Those who enjoy only highly buffed or electroplated blades may view the blade of a kris with condescension, but a kris blade fashioned by a respected *empu* may well be an artistic masterpiece, the work often commanding the highest prices. As the Western world gradually becomes more appreciative of the art of the kris, some of these fine blades will increase enormously in value. Prices of Naga- and Singha[3]-decorated blades are already in-

---

[1] Gold applied using mercury and heat.
[2] Gold applied to a barbed metal surface.
[3] Serpent and lion.

creasing rapidly; accordingly, the wise collector will treat his blades well.

A kris blade is best cleaned by first using strong soap and hot water applied with a stiff brush. After rinsing and drying well, small rust spots may be removed with fine steel wool, more stubborn spots with fine emery paper. The blade is then rubbed with cloth to bring up some sheen and oil is applied. Tradition calls for sandalwood oil but the clove oil used on Japanese blades is equivalent protection. Some collectors like these odours; others prefer an application of fine gun oil wiped into the blade. Museums prefer to use paste wax on arms in general. Clear, hard wax shoe polish is a good choice, particularly if the blade is put on display. It is a different matter, however, if the blade bears much rust or if the contrasting colours in the textured *pamor* can no longer be detected. In smooth Balinese blades, large areas of deep blue-black colour may be worn off, thus making invisible the silvery threads of nickelous metal. In these cases, restoration of the blade must be undertaken. However, not a great amount has been written about redamasking methods for kris blades. There are just a few accounts in English and Malay, some of which verge on alchemy, others specifying materials hard to obtain anywhere other than in South-East Asia. Here is a common procedure for restoring colour to the *pamor* blade of a kris. Note the use of arsenious oxide (arsenic—Malay, *warangan*). It is a poison with deadly toxic effect; therefore, extreme care must be used when handling it.

First clean the blade thoroughly of all grease and dirt using soap and water as described above. Then clean the blade with repeated hard brushings using a brush and lime segments and with frequent rinsing until all traces of rust are gone. Dry the blade thoroughly. Now prepare a mixture of lime juice and powdered white arsenic. Mix sufficient arsenic and one fl. oz. of lime juice to a heavy cream consistency. Using a flat artist's brush with stiff bristles, spread the concoction evenly on the entire kris blade. Then set it aside to dry. Wash out the artist's brush and prepare another fl. oz. of fresh lime juice. Hold the kris vertically, resting its tip in a basin or sink. Starting near the tang, slowly wash down the kris blade with the brush and fresh lime juice. The blade will begin to darken from shades of grey to black, its colour responsive to the rate of application and the amount of lime juice it receives. With some practice the desired shades will be obtained. Rinse the blade thoroughly of the lime juice, and dry and oil it as described earlier. The oil (or wax) coating improves lustre and helps bring out the contrast in the *pamor* markings.

There are many variations on this method of colouring a blade. Any Asian lime seems effective as do Western lemons. Indeed, some kris blades respond to solutions of acetic acid diluted down from 5 per cent white vinegar; others to long soaks in sulphur and salt mixtures followed by treatment with arsenic and limes. Most important, it seems, is absolute cleanliness of the blade prior to the damasking process.

After giving proper attention to its blade, cleaning the decorative metal of a kris logically follows. Although it is best to disassemble a piece prior to cleaning each portion, this is rarely possible—nor is it necessary if care is taken. The cleaning of metals usually requires strong solvents or chemical preparations to remove surface corrosions, some of which are bound to be transferred to adjacent organic surfaces with the necessity of subsequent removal. Therefore, it is best to 'get the dirty work over with' so that the piece can finally be cleaned in its entirety without further interruption.

Prior to detailed work on any piece, a less detailed overall cleaning should be done. Dust and loose dirt can be removed with a brush. Wrattans and woven materials may be further cleaned using a vacuum-cleaner and nozzle attachment but should be protected with a cloth cover (through which the vacuuming is done) to prevent tearing of the fragile materials. Cruddy deposits are removed with a wooden manicure stick or the like to avoid scratching or gouging underlying materials. Portions that are safe from water are then washed using a damp cloth and mild detergent. Baby bath soap is used in museum work because of its neutral acidity factor.

A great amount of the metalwork found in an antique arms collection is in the form of repousse or engraved brass and silver. These are easily cleaned materials and excellent preparations for so doing are available worldwide. The liquid brass cleaners are good cleaners of metals in general as they are effective on aqueous, oily, and greasy deposits regardless of the base metal. Cleaners formulated for cleaning copper only are in a different class and are not recommended for use in the renovation of art objects of the type described here. A liquid brass cleaner may be used safely on iron, brass, or copper. However, it is most effective on brass. It will brighten dull brass to a brilliant light gold colour and, with repeated application, restore old and discoloured brass to a similar appearance. These cleaners are effective on other copper-bearing alloys also. On so-called 'oriental white copper', a hard silvery shine with a faint yellowish tint is produced. With the alloy *suasa* (see p. 21) a truly unusual colour is produced—a distinct pinkish hue. After treatment of these metals with the cleaner, residues should be removed with a wet cloth. A toothbrush covered with the cloth is used to clean out recesses in the work. Then the piece is dried with cloth or paper towels. It may be left out to dry in the open air or its drying may be hastened by using a hair dryer at low-heat setting. Proceed slowly; the metal should not be heated more than warm to the touch.

The cleaning or restoration of silver to its original appearance is surely one of the most satisfying tasks in a collector's life. This noble metal, second only to gold in its illustrious history, is more the metal of the common man expressing his the piece with a cloth or paper towel and set it aside to dry thoroughly. A hair dryer may be used with caution; set for low heat and allow the metal to be warmed only.

Silver which is coated with old tarnish often requires second and third applications of the tarnish remover. With each application the piece gets cleaner and brighter, making the additional work well worth the effort. A piece thoroughly cleaned in its crevices and decorative areas may seem too clean—without colour contrast in these areas—but it will later come right. After one or more subsequent light cleanings which avoid the nooks, crevices, and decorative detail, the piece will take on its full beauty. The large surfaces will be brilliantly displayed and will be accentuated by the contrasting coloration of its decorated areas. Final polishing is done with a jeweller's polishing cloth—a cloth impregnated with jeweller's rouge. This handy material works wonders on dull and scratched silver and gold, restoring the metal to its original surface shine. Care must be taken to avoid softening the corners and edges of newer work. Greater care must be exercised in the polishing of plated work, particularly with repousse items, to avoid removing the plating (gold or silver) from the higher surfaces.

Gold requires far less attention than brass or silver. It is best cleaned with mild soap and water followed by a polish with a jeweller's cloth. For gold that has accumulated stubborn dirt deposits, the solvent action of liquid silver polish is effective as are weak alcohol and water preparations. Care must be used when cleaning Malay gold contrasted with red tamarind stains. Water alone is the only safe cleaner for such pieces. Gold or silver applied in the fire-gilding process and in some *koftgari* techniques is exceedingly thin. Such areas should be cleaned most gently using a damp cloth, a mild cleaning agent, and the tip of a finger.

Hard organic materials—ivory, horn, and wood—are easier to renovate than metals. These materials are also best cleaned need to enjoy some special privilege. Silver was (and is) widely available, easily worked, and not subject to royal prohibitions of use. It satisfies everyone's desire for ready decoration at low cost. The owning and care of silver is a lively relationship in that one's joy with its appearance is renewed many times in a lifetime. Each loving period with polish and polishing cloth ends with renewed contemplation of the beauty that has been revealed. When pieces are heavily tarnished with a blue-black coating, the transformation is simply magnificent.

Of course gold itself is noble, splendid, and expensive but in its changelessness it has acquired an austerity and aloofness that defies its owner to disturb it in any way. It needs little attention except to occasionally have atmospheric residue removed from its pristine surface. Gold is more decorative; silver both decorative and utilitarian. With gold comes the satisfaction of owning the best; with silver is realized the love of a responsive metal.

Many silver cleaners are available to the collector and all provide satisfying results when properly applied. Paste-type cleaners have more abrasive content than liquid cleaners, and they are most useful when initially cleaning a heavily tarnished article. Liquid cleaners do well when used to maintain the polish of previously cleaned items. Apply the paste with a damp cloth. Work it well into nooks, crannies, the recesses of repousse and engraved work, into wire filigree, and around the mounts of gemstones. Allow the paste to start its chemical action. In a few minutes proceed with the cleaning using a damp cloth for larger surfaces and a toothbrush covered with that cloth for recesses. If the piece is heavily tarnished, cleaning out the recesses will be a slow process. Use a toothbrush or manicure stick wrapped in the cloth for all tiny spaces. Now rinse the entire piece using the cloth and toothbrush as described. It is important to remove all of the residue from the crevices before it dries out and sets into whitish deposits. Dry using a damp cloth, soft toothbrush, and wooden manicure stick but more care must be used in the application of a detergent. Baby bath soap and water are again recommended. The piece must not be allowed to absorb much water as it may swell or crack and subsequent drying may prove difficult. Old wrattans, fibres, and cloth are delicate indeed and are best left without further attention after a gentle cleaning with a dry brush.

Repairs to hard organic materials are rather easily made although, in practice, not always made neatly. Common liquid white glue works well in all cases. The trick is to keep it in place without messy runs which harden into unsightly globs. The area to be repaired should be cleaned and almost dry. Apply the white glue with a manicure stick or a toothpick, working it well into cracks or spreading it on both surfaces. Press or squeeze the parts together and wipe off the excess glue with a damp cloth. Now apply rubber bands or tape to hold the parts closely while the glue is drying. Position the piece so the glue cannot run out of the repaired joint. This procedure usually provides a perfect repair as the white glue is an ideal bonding material for organic substances. Also it becomes nearly transparent with little surface gloss after hardening, thus being quite undetectable in the repaired piece.

Hand polishing with a soft cloth is often sufficient beauty care for these materials, but often something more is needed to heighten the natural lustre or bring out the grain. Furniture wax is a good substance to use; on wooden items try to obtain a type without additives. Museums use a micro-crystalline wax in paste form, an acid-free wax which polishes easily and has high protective value. The surfaces of natural woods can be renovated using very fine steel wool, furniture wax, and much hard rubbing. Ivory with a dull finish is best restored with tooth powder—certainly a logical choice. Lacquer is best restored by application of powdered rottenstone on a wet cloth. Unsightly breaks and cracks can often be camouflaged by judicious use of artist's oil colours in an appropriate earth-tone shade. A small amount of suitable colour is wiped into the contrasting portion of the broken piece until a good colour match is obtained. Damaged areas of gold and silver can be similarly repaired with the use of gilding waxes available at art supply shops.

*     *     *

In our description of the kris and its many aspects, we have, in this little book, resurrected six hundred years of detail, picked out what is best said in such short form and entrusted to the reader his judgement of our work. His pleasure is our reward and should he be inspired to go further than this scant volume, we will become his eager readers.

# Select Bibliography

Bronson, B., 'Terrestrial and Meteoric Nickel in the Indonesian Keris', *Journal of the Historical Metallurgy Society*, London, Vol. 21, No. 1, July 1987.

Burkhill, I. H., *Dictionary of Economic Products of the Malay Peninsula*, Kuala Lumpur.

Clifford, H., *In Court and Kampong*, London, 1897.

Cool, Capt. W., *The Dutch in the East–the Lombock Expedition*, 1897.

Crawfurd, J., *History of the Indian Archipelago*, Edinburgh, 1820.

Darmosugito, *Serba Sedikit Tentang Soal Keris*, Jakarta, 1942.

Gardner, G. B., *Keris and other Malay Weapons*, Singapore, 1936.

Goloubew, V., *L'age du Bronze au Tonkin*, Hanoi, 1929.

Groneman, J., *Der Kris der Javaner*, Yogyakarta, 1910.

Hamzuri, *Petunjuk Singkat Tentang Keris*, Jakarta, National Museum Publication, 1982.

Harrisson, Tom, 'A Golden Kris Handle from Balingian, Sarawak', *Journal of the Malaysian Branch of the Royal Asiatic Society*, Vol. XXXIX, 1967.

Hill, A. H., 'The Keris and other Malay Weapons', *Journal of the Malayan Branch of the Royal Asiatic Society*, Vol. XXIX, Pt. 4, 1956.

Holstein, P., *Contribution à l'Etude des Armes Orientales*, Paris, 1930.

Jasper, J. E., and Mas Pirngadie, *De Inlandsche Kunst Nijverheid in Nederlandsch-Indie*, Vol. V, The Hague, 1930.

Kennedy, M. A., *A History of Malaya*, Liverpool, 1960.

Koesni, *Pakam Pengetahuan Tentang Keris*, Semarang, 1979.

Krieger, H. W., *Primitive Weapons and Armor of the Philippine Islands*, Washington, 1926.

Kronholz, J., 'Magic Sword', *Wall Street Journal*, 29 September 1983.

McNair, J. F. A., *Perak and the Malays: Sarong and Keris*, London, 1878; reprinted Kuala Lumpur, University of Malaya Press, 1972.

Middleton, H., *Voyage to the Moluccas*, 1604.

Newbold, T. J., *British Settlements in the Straits of Malacca*, Kuala Lumpur, Oxford University Press, 1971.

Ostmeier, J. J. B., *Voor den Pandhuisdienst*, Batavia (Jakarta), Albrecht Pub., 1911.

Raffles, T. S., *The History of Java*, London, 1817; reprinted Kuala Lumpur, Oxford University Press, 1978 and 1988.

Ramseyer, Urs, *The Art and Culture of Bali*, Office du Livre S. A., 1977; reprinted Singapore, Oxford University Press, 1986.

Rassers, W. H., *Panji, the Culture Hero*, The Hague, Martinus Nijhoff, 1959.

Shahrum bin Yub, *Keris dan Senjata² Pendek*, Kuala Lumpur, 1967.

Skeat, W. W., *Malay Magic*, London, 1900; reprinted Singapore, Oxford University Press, 1984.

Solyum, G. B., *The World of the Javanese Keris*, Honolulu, East-West Center, 1978.

Thomson, Garry, *The Museum Environment*, London, 1986.

Van Ness, Edward C., and Prawirohardjo, S., *Javanese Wayang Kulit*, Kuala Lumpur, Oxford University Press, 1980.

Wallace, A. R., *The Malay Archipelago*, 1869; reprinted Singapore, Oxford University Press, 1986.

Woodman, D., *The Republic of Indonesia*, New York, 1955.

Wray, L., *Papers on Malay Subjects*, Kuala Lumpur, 1925.

de Zoete, Beryl, and Spies, Walter, *Dance and Drama in Bali*, London, 1938; reprinted Kuala Lumpur, Oxford University Press, 1982.

# Index

INDEX